Spelling
Workbook

Siegfried Engelmann

mheducation.com/prek-12

Copyright © 2021 McGraw-Hill Education

All rights reserved. No part of this publication may be reproduced or distributed in any form or by any means, or stored in a database or retrieval system, without the prior written consent of McGraw-Hill Education, including, but not limited to, network storage or transmission, or broadcast for distance learning.

Send all inquiries to:
McGraw-Hill Education
8787 Orion Place
Columbus, OH 43240

ISBN: 978-0-07-905379-4
MHID: 0-07-905379-3

Printed in the United States of America.

3 4 5 6 7 8 9 10 WEB 26 25 24 23 22 21

Name _____ 1

A

thought   worth   match   use   power   reason

B

1. _____ mist   3. _____ handle   5. _____ restless
2. _____ misprint   4. _____ mishandle   6. _____ handleless

C

1. _____   4. _____
2. _____   5. _____
3. _____   6. _____

D

1. Some wild berries contane poison.   _____
2. Phisical exercise helps your body's development.   _____
3. Both sience and writing classes are featuring a panel of speakers.   _____

END OF LESSON 1

Lesson 1

2 Name _____

A

doubt   mother   print   place   price   view

B

1. _____ power
2. _____ powerful
3. _____ thoughtful
4. _____ doubtless
5. _____ motherless
6. _____ misuse

C

1. _____
2. _____
3. _____
4. _____
5. _____
6. _____

D

1. The union of trucks formed a protetive wall.   _____
2. There are many dutys as a science teacher.   _____
3. He used logic to solve a magor crime.   _____

END OF LESSON 2

Lesson 2

Name _____

3

A

b u a k t m i s o r g e i f

B

cover   like   cure   move   fresh   serve

C

1. _____ reason   3. _____ coverless   5. _____ printable
2. _____ reasonable   4. _____ mother   6. _____ powerless

D

1. _____   3. _____
2. _____   4. _____

E

These words are in the word search. Circle 7 or more of the words.

brown	vein	lose
win	breathe	fault
spent	source	quick
many	swim	trend

b s s v w t f
q r s p v r a
u l o s e e u
i q u w i n l
c e r i n d t
k o c m a n y
b r e a t h e

END OF LESSON 3

Lesson 3

4

Name _____

A

sound　　　quote　　　guide　　　name　　　base　　　sore

B

1. _____ + _____ = reasonable
2. _____ + _____ + _____ = returnable
3. _____ + _____ = remove
4. _____ + _____ = worthless
5. _____ + _____ = misshape
6. _____ + _____ + _____ = resourceful
7. _____ + _____ = misquote
8. _____ + _____ = powerful

C

Make a small **v** above every vowel letter.
Make a small **c** above every consonant letter.

n　e　i　f　o　b　u　c　t　p　a　d　h　i　m　e　o

D

Cross out the misspelled words in these sentences.
Then write the words correctly above the crossed-out words.

Meny people where late.

Maby thay need sum help.

Lesson 4

E These words are in the word search.
Circle 7 or more of the words.

replace	hope	sneak
niece	note	length
sleeve	leave	listen
last	little	fence

```
b  l  i  s  t  e  n
c  l  i  h  n  r  m
l  a  s  t  o  e  s
e  l  n  r  t  p  l
n  z  e  i  e  l  e
g  r  a  a  e  a  e
t  i  k  e  v  c  v
h  f  e  n  c  e  e
```

F Each sentence has one misspelled word.
Write each word correctly on the blank.

1. I hope you retain your pashion for science. _____

2. She was regresing instead of getting better. _____

3. Playing lojic games makes me tense. _____

Lesson 5 is a test lesson. There is no worksheet.

Lesson 4   5

6 Name _____

A

1. _____   5. _____
2. _____   6. _____
3. _____   7. _____
4. _____   8. _____

B

1. like + able   = _____
2. like + ness   = _____
3. cheer + ful   = _____
4. price + less   = _____
5. guide + ing   = _____
6. hope + ing   = _____
7. hope + less   = _____
8. quote + able   = _____

C. Fill in the blanks to show the morphographs in each word.

1. _____ + _____ = powerful
2. _____ + _____ = reserve
3. _____ + _____ + _____ = remarkable
4. _____ + _____ + _____ = helplessness
5. _____ + _____ + _____ = painfulness
6. _____ + _____ = report

D. Cross out the misspelled words in these sentences. Then write the words correctly above the crossed-out words.

I though they were helples.

We found a plase with a restfull view.

END OF LESSON 6

7

Name _____

A

breath   fashion   fair   solve   source   tribe

B

1. stage + ing = _____
2. time + less = _____
3. cure + able = _____
4. firm + ness = _____
5. serve + ing = _____
6. use + less = _____
7. fear + ful = _____
8. trace + ed = _____

C

Nineteen athletes exercised throughout the morning.

_____

_____

D

1. _____   4. _____
2. _____   5. _____
3. _____   6. _____

Lesson 7

E Fill in the blanks to show the morphographs in each word.

1. _____ + _____ = resource
2. _____ + _____ + _____ = helplessness
3. _____ + _____ + _____ = returning
4. _____ + _____ = faithful
5. _____ + _____ + _____ = refillable
6. _____ + _____ + _____ = youthfulness

END OF LESSON 7

8 Name _____

A

_ _ _ e _ _ _ _   _ _ h l e _ e _

_ x _ _ c _ s _ _   _ _ _ o u _ _ _ _

_ _ _   _ o _ _ i _ _ .

_____

_____

B

1. grab   3. win   5. drip   7. art   9. slip   11. run
2. reason   4. move   6. star   8. water   10. plan   12. poison

C   Add the morphographs together.
Some of the words follow the rule about dropping the final e.

1. name + ed   = _____

2. solve + ing   = _____

3. sore + ness   = _____

4. guide + ed   = _____

5. fashion + able   = _____

6. price + ing   = _____

7. price + less   = _____

8. use + ful   = _____

9. re + place + ing   = _____

10. use + ed   = _____

Lesson 8

D Write the correct word for each sentence.

1. Did you **here/hear** me? _____
2. Please put these over **there/their.** _____
3. Thank you **vary/very** much. _____
4. The cat is licking its **tale/tail.** _____
5. There is a **hole/whole** in my shoe. _____
6. Will you **loan/lone** me some money? _____
7. That answer is **write/right.** _____
8. I'm chewing a **peace/piece** of gum. _____

E Fill in the blanks to show the morphographs in each word.

1. _____ + _____ = recover
2. _____ + _____ + _____ = refreshing
3. _____ + _____ = fairness
4. _____ + _____ + _____ = painfulness
5. _____ + _____ + _____ = misspelling
6. _____ + _____ = workable

F Each sentence has one misspelled word. Write each word correctly on the blank.

1. The vase is brakeable, so handle it carefully. _____
2. I doubt if the cure is as painfull as the disease. _____
3. Mother likes to quote reasenable advice from others. _____

END OF LESSON 8

9 Name ____

A

rich   globe   sign   value   store   scribe

B

_ _ _ _ _ _   _ _ _ _ _ _

_ _ _ _ _ _ _   _ _ _ _ _ _ _

_ _ _   _ _ _ _ _ _ .

_____

_____

C

1. _____   4. _____
2. _____   5. _____
3. _____   6. _____

D

1. wonder   4. big   7. cover   10. mad
2. best   5. skin   8. scar   11. brother
3. drip   6. kind   9. trip   12. hop

12   Lesson 9

E Add these morphographs together.
Some of the words follow the rule about dropping the final e.

1. value + able = _____
2. solve + ing = _____
3. re + source + ful = _____
4. un + fair + ness = _____
5. shame + less = _____
6. like + ed = _____
7. have + ing = _____

F Write the correct word for each sentence. If you're not sure of a word, look it up in the list of homonyms on pages 211–213.

1. My **feat/feet** itch. _____
2. Most countries want **peace/piece**. _____
3. Do you like this **weather/whether**? _____
4. This desk is made from **wood/would**. _____
5. Our room is **to/too** cold. _____
6. We passed **threw/through** the tunnel. _____

G Each sentence has one misspelled word. Write each word correctly on the blank.

1. Mary is doubtfull about returning as a guide next year. _____
2. I thought the shirt was returnible because the price was still on it. _____
3. Move the fresh flowers to a safer plase. _____

Lesson 10 is a test lesson. There is no worksheet.

Lesson 9   13

11 Name _____

A

1. _____
   _____

2. _____
   _____

B

length   strength   fright   tough   short   loose

C

1. stop + ing   = _____
2. sad + ness   = _____
3. reason + ing = _____
4. plan + ed   = _____
5. hop + ing   = _____
6. star + less   = _____
7. snug + ness   = _____
8. pain + ful   = _____

D

valuable	replace	reason	helplessness
fashion	guide	scribe	breathless
thoughtful	powerless	solving	signal

E

Add the morphographs together.
Some of the words follow the rule about dropping the final e.

1. serve + ing = _____
2. store + ed = _____
3. hope + ful = _____
4. hope + ing = _____
5. smile + ing = _____
6. ripe + est = _____
7. doubt + less = _____
8. prove + ing = _____

F

Each sentence has one misspelled word.
Write each word correctly on the blank.

1. It would be pointless to hire him if he misspells and missfiles things. _____
2. A portable radio still needs power to make sownd. _____
3. My back is soar from having a sleepless night. _____

END OF LESSON 11

A

cvc + v

1. trap + ed = _____

2. big + est = _____

3. spot + less = _____

4. wonder + ful = _____

5. slip + ed = _____

6. step + ing = _____

7. mother + ing = _____

8. sad + est = _____

B

Cross out the misspelled words in these sentences.
Then write the words correctly above the crossed-out words.

The juge was resonable and fare.

Someone plased a sine on the stor.

C These words are in the word search. Circle 9 or more of the words.

choicest	bridge	loose
live	read	break
house	solve	shops
greatest	pool	tent
seek	ruling	

```
c  b  r  i  d  g  e  g
s  h  b  r  e  a  k  r
p  o  o  l  o  o  s  e
r  u  l  i  n  g  h  a
r  s  s  v  c  t  o  t
e  e  e  e  e  e  p  e
c  h  a  e  o  n  s  s
p  o  o  d  k  t  t  t
```

END OF LESSON 12

Lesson 12   17

13 Name _____

A

People weren't interested in the photograph.

_____

_____

B

1. _____

   _____

2. _____

   _____

C

1. wander + ing = _____

2. snap + ed   = _____

3. swim + er   = _____

4. flat + ness   = _____

5. win + er   = _____

6. step + ed   = _____

7. great + est   = _____

8. skid + ing   = _____

D Circle the misspelled word in each group.
Then write it correctly on the line.

1. powerful
   signal
   shoper
   review
   _____

2. hopefull
   source
   place
   restless
   _____

3. uncover
   scribe
   formal
   fashun
   _____

4. morning
   breth
   unfair
   globe
   _____

E Add the morphographs together.
Some of the words follow the rule about dropping the final e.

1. tribe + al = _____
2. fine + er = _____
3. life + less = _____
4. fine + al = _____
5. cure + able = _____
6. time + less = _____
7. globe + al = _____
8. rage + ing = _____

F Each sentence has one misspelled word.
Write each word correctly on the blank.

1. Be careful not to misquote her or missuse her name. _____
2. I like to surve in a tennis match. _____

END OF LESSON 13

14 Name _____

A

firm   script   verse   tone   part   frost

B

__ e o __ __ __ __   __ __ __ __ n ' __

__ __ __ e r __ __ __ __ __   __ __   __ __ __

p h __ __ o __ __ __ __ p __ .

_____

_____

C

1. _____ + _____ = _____

2. _____ + _____ = _____

3. _____ + _____ = _____

4. _____ + _____ = _____

5. _____ + _____ = _____

6. _____ + _____ = _____

D Circle the misspelled word in each group. Then write it correctly on the line.

1. tough
   gide
   helpless
   formal
   _____

2. greatest
   fright
   lenght
   unhappy
   _____

3. useles
   widest
   sounded
   straining
   _____

4. scribe
   valueable
   resource
   reserve
   _____

Lesson 15 is a test lesson. There is no worksheet.

16 Name

A

crease   shrink   change   press   claim   quest

B

_ _ _ _ _   _ _ _ _ _ _
_ _ _ _ _ _ _ _ _   _ _
_ _ _   _ _ _ _ _ _ _ _ _ .

C

1. _____   4. _____
2. _____   5. _____
3. _____   6. _____

D Add the morphographs together.
Some of the words follow the final-e rule.

1. peace + ful = _____
2. hope + less = _____
3. take + ing = _____
4. fine + al = _____
5. re + fine + ed = _____
6. large + est = _____
7. crease + ed = _____
8. loose + en = _____
9. lone + ly = _____
10. hide + ing = _____

END OF LESSON 16

A

strict   create   tense   state   treat   govern

B

1. _____

2. _____

C

1. happy + ness = _____
2. try + ed = _____
3. play + ful = _____
4. pity + ful = _____
5. carry + ing = _____
6. carry + ed = _____
7. say + ing = _____
8. worry + er = _____

D

| ly | mad | ness | fine | ripe | er | est |

1. _____
2. _____
3. _____
4. _____
5. _____

6. _____
7. _____
8. _____
9. _____

E Add the morphographs together. Some of the words follow the final-e rule. Some of them follow the doubling rule.

1. hope + ful = _____
2. hope + ing = _____
3. hop + ing = _____
4. globe + al = _____
5. de + fine + ing = _____
6. snug + est = _____
7. wonder + ful = _____
8. loose + ly = _____
9. sad + ness = _____
10. slip + ing = _____
11. un + re + solve + able = _____
12. mad + ly = _____

F Each sentence has one misspelled word.
Write each word correctly on the blank.

1. Nineteen athleates raced through the streets. _____

2. How did you recover from that remarkable feet? _____

3. I was hopping to hear your report. _____

END OF LESSON 17

Name _____ 18

A

1. _____   4. _____
2. _____   5. _____
3. _____   6. _____

B Change y when consonant-and-y + anything except i.

Add the morphographs together.
Some of the words follow the rule about changing **y** to **i**.

1. sturdy + ness   = _____
2. dry + ing   = _____
3. carry + ed   = _____
4. fancy + est   = _____
5. play + ing   = _____
6. pity + ful   = _____
7. nasty + est   = _____
8. study + ing   = _____

Lesson 18   27

C Make 9 real words from the morphographs in the box.

| less | star | ing | hope | ed | use | spot |

1. _____
2. _____
3. _____
4. _____
5. _____
6. _____
7. _____
8. _____
9. _____

D Write the correct word for each sentence. If you're not sure of a word, look it up in the list of homonyms on pages 211–213.

1. Fifteen minus seven is **ate/eight.** _____
2. **Meet/Meat** me after school. _____
3. **Wear/Where** are you going? _____
4. That was quite a **tail/tale** Sandy told. _____
5. The runners **vary/very** their speed. _____
6. Do the books go **their/there?** _____
7. Turn **right/write** at the sign. _____
8. I finished the **hole/whole** report. _____

E Each sentence has one misspelled word. Write each word correctly on the blank.

1. The weather will very across the globe. _____
2. You'll get used to the sorness in your feet. _____

END OF LESSON 18

Name

A

Anybody would rather be healthy instead of rich.

_____

_____

B

1. _____ + _____ = _____
2. _____ + _____ = _____
3. _____ + _____ = _____
4. _____ + _____ = _____
5. _____ + _____ = _____
6. _____ + _____ = _____

C

1. _____   5. _____
2. _____   6. _____
3. _____   7. _____
4. _____   8. _____

Lesson 19

D Fill in the blanks to show the morphographs in each word.

1. _____ + _____ + _____ + _____ = unreformed
2. _____ + _____ + _____ = departed
3. _____ + _____ + _____ + _____ = misreported
4. _____ + _____ + _____ + _____ = unconfirmed
5. _____ + _____ + _____ = reinstate
6. _____ + _____ + _____ = helplessly
7. _____ + _____ + _____ = restfully
8. _____ + _____ = resource
9. _____ + _____ + _____ = frightening
10. _____ + _____ + _____ = uselessness
11. _____ + _____ + _____ = confronted
12. _____ + _____ + _____ = delights

E Each sentence has one misspelled word. Write each word correctly on the blank.

1. I liked reading the tail even with its misspellings.   _____
2. The briteness of her smile makes her very likable.   _____
3. This fashionable piece of furniture is timeles.   _____

Lesson 20 is a test lesson. There is no worksheet.

Lesson 19

Name

A

_ _ _ _ o _ _ _ o _ _ _ _ _ _ _ _ _

_ _ _ e a _ _ _ _ _ _ e a _ _ _

_ _ _ _ .

_____

_____

B

straight   found   settle   agree   claim

C

1. _____ + _____ = facing
2. _____ + _____ = running
3. _____ + _____ = happiness
4. _____ + _____ = swimmer
5. _____ + _____ = valuable
6. _____ + _____ + _____ = reserved
7. _____ + _____ = pitiful
8. _____ + _____ + _____ = exchanging

Lesson 21

D

1. _____ + _____ = _____
2. _____ + _____ = _____
3. _____ + _____ = _____
4. _____ + _____ = _____
5. _____ + _____ = _____
6. _____ + _____ = _____

E Cross out the misspelled words in these sentences.
Then write the words correctly above the crossed-out words.

Are you intrested in incresing your strenht?

There are ninteen people in the photegraph.

F Each sentence has one misspelled word.
Write each word correctly on the blank.

1. The farmer was hopful that he would have the biggest peppers. _____

2. The saddest part of the skirpt is coming up soon. _____

3. The people in the photograph wernt smiling. _____

END OF LESSON 21

Name _____ **22**

A

___ ___ ___ ___ ___ ___ ___ ___ ___ ___ ___ ___ ___ ___ ___ ___ ___
___ ___ ___ ___ ___ ___ ___ ___ ___ ___ ___ ___ ___ ___ ___ ___ ___ ___
___ ___ ___ ___ .

_____

_____

B

prove   cause   great   text   spirit   thirst

C **Figure out the rules and write them.**
Remember to spell the words correctly.

with anything except **i** . . . **i** in a word when the . . . the next morphograph begins . . . change the **y** to . . . word ends consonant-and-**y** and

_____

_____

word when the next . . . final **e** from a . . . with **v** . . . drop the . . . morphograph begins

_____

_____

D

1. win   2. low   3. swim   4. chew   5. draw

Lesson 22   33

E Add the morphographs together.
Some of the words follow the rule about changing u to i.

1. stray + ed = _____

2. cry + ing = _____

3. worry + ed = _____

4. nasty + er = _____

5. pity + ing = _____

6. deny + al = _____

7. try + al = _____

8. play + ful = _____

F Fill in the blanks to show the morphographs in each word.
Remember to spell each morphograph correctly.

1. _____ + _____ = starring
2. _____ + _____ + _____ = reserved
3. _____ + _____ = final
4. _____ + _____ = happiest
5. _____ + _____ = sadden
6. _____ + _____ + _____ = resourceful
7. _____ + _____ + _____ = exchanging
8. _____ + _____ = lucky

END OF LESSON 22

Name _____ **23**

A

1. _____
   _____

2. _____
   _____

B

**Write the correct spelling for each word.
Then write one of these letters after each number.**

Write **O** if the word is spelled by just putting the morphographs together.
Write **A** if the final-**e** rule explains why the spelling is changed.
Write **B** if the doubling rule explains why the spelling is changed.
Write **C** if the **y**-to-**i** rule explains why the spelling is changed.

1. _____ vary + ed   = _____
2. _____ sad + ness   = _____
3. _____ tense + ion   = _____
4. _____ play + ful   = _____
5. _____ prove + en   = _____
6. _____ swim + er   = _____
7. _____ low + est   = _____
8. _____ pity + ful   = _____
9. _____ settle + ment = _____
10. _____ change + ing = _____

Lesson 23   35

C Add the morphographs together.
Remember: The morphograph y is a vowel letter.

1. rate + ion = _____
2. treat + ment = _____
3. con + text = _____
4. re + in + state = _____
5. edge + y = _____
6. wreck + age = _____
7. con + fine + ment = _____
8. ease + y = _____
9. pro + claim + ed = _____
10. in + crease + ing = _____

D Figure out the rules and write them.

word when the next morphograph . . . drop the final **e** from a . . . begins with **v**

_____

_____

a short word when the . . . the next morphograph begins with **v** . . . word ends **cvc** and . . . double the final **c** in

_____

_____

END OF LESSON 23

Name _____

24

A

1. _____
_____

2. _____
_____

B

1. _____
2. _____
3. _____

4. _____
5. _____
6. _____

C

1. _____
2. _____
3. _____

4. _____
5. _____

D Write the correct spelling for each word.
Then write one of these letters after each number.

Write **O** if the word is spelled by just putting the morphographs together.
Write **A** if the final-**e** rule explains why the spelling is changed.
Write **B** if the doubling rule explains why the spelling is changed.
Write **C** if the **y**-to-**i** rule explains why the spelling is changed.

1. _____ poison + ed = _____
2. _____ hurry + ed = _____
3. _____ carry + ing = _____
4. _____ trap + er = _____
5. _____ happy + ness = _____
6. _____ ease + y = _____
7. _____ proud + ly = _____
8. _____ late + ly = _____
9. _____ tense + ion = _____
10. _____ clap + ing = _____

E Each sentence has one misspelled word.
Write each word correctly on the blank.

1. I'd be surprised if anybody ate that meet. _____
2. All of the reckage from the boats floated inland. _____
3. Which rocks are you useing? _____

Lesson 25 is a test lesson. There is no worksheet.

Name _____

A Write the correct spelling for each word.
Then write one of these letters after each number.

Write **O** if the word is spelled by just putting the morphographs together.
Write **A** if the final-**e** rule explains why the spelling is changed.
Write **B** if the doubling rule explains why the spelling is changed.
Write **C** if the **y**-to-**i** rule explains why the spelling is changed.

1. _____ low + er = _____
2. _____ snap + ed = _____
3. _____ store + age = _____
4. _____ edge + y = _____
5. _____ slip + ing = _____
6. _____ move + ment = _____
7. _____ fit + ness = _____
8. _____ flaw + ed = _____
9. _____ note + ion = _____
10. _____ play + ing = _____
11. _____ run + y = _____
12. _____ like + able = _____

B Circle the misspelled word in each group. Then write it correctly on the line.

1. fashion
   poison
   strate
   rather
   _____

2. glory
   pleaze
   place
   settle
   _____

3. brother
   wrong
   carry
   hopeing
   _____

4. prove
   cawse
   hurried
   agree
   _____

5. crease
   change
   request
   ninteen
   _____

6. choice
   sorce
   strength
   studying
   _____

7. sturdyness
   recover
   serve
   priceless
   _____

8. swimmer
   serving
   pitiful
   lowwer
   _____

C Fill in the blanks to show the morphographs in each word.

1. _____ + _____ + _____ = repressive
2. _____ + _____ + _____ = depression
3. _____ + _____ + _____ = expressed
4. _____ + _____ = feature
5. _____ + _____ + _____ = defeated
6. _____ + _____ = passion
7. _____ + _____ + _____ = profoundly
8. _____ + _____ + _____ = invaluable

END OF LESSON 26

Name _____

A
Write s or es in the second column.
Then add the morphographs together.

1. press + _____ = _____
2. shop + _____ = _____
3. buzz + _____ = _____
4. box + _____ = _____
5. stretch + _____ = _____
6. rich + _____ = _____
7. wash + _____ = _____
8. script + _____ = _____

B

1. _____
   _____

2. _____
   _____

C

1. _____   4. _____
2. _____   5. _____
3. _____

D Write the correct word for each sentence.

1. The **weather/whether** has been great. _____
2. They found **their/there** things. _____
3. We **through/threw** rocks in the lake. _____
4. Pete ate **to/too** much. _____
5. Please bring those books **hear/here**. _____
6. I've never heard such a strange **tail/tale**. _____

E Fill in the blanks to show the morphographs in each word.

1. _____ + _____ = poisonous
2. _____ + _____ = famous
3. _____ + _____ = relate
4. _____ + _____ + _____ = relative
5. _____ + _____ + _____ = reaction
6. _____ + _____ + _____ = expression

F Each sentence has one misspelled word. Write each word correctly on the blank.

1. The peaceful dogs became playfull when I began studying. _____
2. Todd tried to straighten up the storaje room. _____
3. She tried to press the crease out of the pakage. _____

END OF LESSON 27

Name _____

A

    duty   danger   round   speak   fury   seize

B

1. _____
   _____

2. _____
   _____

C

1. _____   4. _____
2. _____   5. _____
3. _____

D Write s or es in the second column.
Then add the morphographs together.

1. tax + _____ = _____
2. brush + _____ = _____
3. claim + _____ = _____
4. waltz + _____ = _____
5. pass + _____ = _____
6. light + _____ = _____
7. reach + _____ = _____
8. rich + _____ = _____

Lesson 28   43

E Add the morphographs together.

1. deny + al = _____
2. glory + ous = _____
3. press + ure = _____
4. mis + con + cept + ion = _____
5. ex + cept + ion = _____
6. flaw + ed = _____
7. thirst + y = _____
8. ex + press + ion = _____
9. in + ject + ion = _____
10. seize + ure = _____

F Each sentence has one misspelled word. Write each word correctly on the blank.

1. You should darken the definning lines to create shadows. _____
2. You can make a helthy treat by drying some fruit. _____
3. She has remarkable skils, but she dresses poorly. _____

END OF LESSON 28

Name _____

29

A

1. _____ 4. _____
2. _____ 5. _____
3. _____

B

C Make 9 real words from the morphographs in the box.

> est   mad   happy   ly   wide   ness   fine

1. _____ 6. _____
2. _____ 7. _____
3. _____ 8. _____
4. _____ 9. _____
5. _____

Lesson 29 **45**

D Fill in the blanks to show the morphographs in each word.

1. _____ + _____ + _____ = protective
2. _____ + _____ + _____ = injected
3. _____ + _____ + _____ = progressed
4. _____ + _____ + _____ = reception
5. _____ + _____ = texture
6. _____ + _____ + _____ = featuring
7. _____ + _____ = passion
8. _____ + _____ = studying
9. _____ + _____ = studious
10. _____ + _____ = signal

E Each sentence has one misspelled word. Write each word correctly on the blank.

1. I agree that we need a speedy settelment. _____
2. Latley I'm so hurried that I'm running around all the time. _____
3. The pressure of a courtroom triel worried her. _____

Lesson 30 is a test lesson. There is no worksheet.

Name _____

A

The union of physical science and logic was a major development.

_____

_____

B

1. worry + _____ = _____
2. play + _____ = _____
3. try   + _____ = _____
4. joy   + _____ = _____
5. copy + _____ = _____
6. boy   + _____ = _____
7. story + _____ = _____
8. study + _____ = _____
9. stay + _____ = _____
10. duty + _____ = _____

C

1. _____   4. _____
2. _____   5. _____
3. _____

Lesson 31   **47**

D Add the morphographs together.
Remember to use your spelling rules.

1. danger + ous = _____
2. seize + ure = _____
3. fury + ous = _____
4. script + ure = _____
5. quest + ion + able = _____
6. poison + ous = _____
7. fur + y = _____
8. please + ure = _____
9. friend + ly + ness = _____
10. re + fuse + al = _____

E Cross out the misspelled words in these sentences.
Then write the words correctly above the crossed-out words.

Could you speak a little lowder, please?

Where are the fameous people?

Their was no reeson for the rejection.

END OF LESSON 31

32

A

___ ___i_o_ __ __y_s____
____e_c_ ___ __og__ ___ _
__jo_ ___e__o____.

_____

_____

B

1. _____
2. _____
3. _____
4. _____
5. _____
6. _____
7. _____
8. _____

C Write s or es in the second column.
Then add the morphographs together.

1. boy + _____ = _____

2. story + _____ = _____

3. try + _____ = _____

4. worry + _____ = _____

5. baby + _____ = _____

6. fly + _____ = _____

7. berry + _____ = _____

8. carry + _____ = _____

D

1. _____

2. _____

3. _____

4. _____

5. _____

E

These words are in the word search. Circle 7 or more of the words.

poison   found   photo
pound   concept flat
lone   pity   whose
store   fact   proven

```
p  p  w  h  o  s  e  f
p  o  i  s  o  n  s  p
c  o  n  c  e  p  t  r
f  o  u  n  d  h  o  o
a  l  o  n  e  o  r  v
c  p  a  r  d  t  e  e
t  p  i  t  y  o  e  n
```

F

Each sentence has one misspelled word. Write each word correctly on the blank.

1. She studyed the statement and then changed her mind. _____

2. He explaned how to turn on the lights in the building. _____

3. The treatment has been proofen to cause rashes. _____

END OF LESSON 32

33 Name

A

__ ____ __ _____ _____ ___ _____ ___ __ ____ _____.

_____

_____

B

1. _____
2. _____
3. _____
4. _____
5. _____
6. _____

C Write s or es in the second column. Then add the morphographs together.

1. worry + _____ = _____
2. pinch + _____ = _____
3. truck + _____ = _____
4. story + _____ = _____
5. stay + _____ = _____
6. copy + _____ = _____
7. poison + _____ = _____
8. study + _____ = _____
9. boy + _____ = _____
10. cry + _____ = _____

D Each sentence has one misspelled word. Write each word correctly on the blank.

1. The goverment was completely receptive to our cause.   _____
2. You'll need to drive strait when you reach the lights.   _____
3. The treatment that Tim was to receive woryed him.   _____

E. Complete the sentences correctly with these words:

whole   write   hole   features   varies   right   weather   morning

1. Caron's experiment failed, but she had the _____ idea.

2. Tony is going to _____ a short story.

3. Our boat won't float because it has a large _____ in it.

4. I can't eat a _____ cake.

5. Murphy's Cafe _____ fried chicken every Friday.

6. Robin exercises every _____ .

7. The _____ in Trinidad rarely _____ .

8. Tahiti _____ great _____ .

END OF LESSON 33

Name _____ **34**

A

1. _____
   _____

2. _____
   _____

B

order   style   count   type   tour   beauty

C

Circle each short word that ends in cvc.

Remember: The letters **y** and **w** are vowel letters at the end of a morphograph.
The letter **x** acts like two consonant letters.
Short words have 3 or 4 letters.

1. gain
2. know
3. spin
4. spirit
5. fur
6. show
7. boy
8. swim
9. box
10. trap
11. brother
12. win
13. drip
14. tax
15. flop
16. cover

Lesson 34

D Add the morphographs together. Be careful. Some of the words follow 2 spelling rules.

1. edge + y + ness = _____
2. lone + ly + est = _____
3. re + cept + ion = _____
4. beauty + ful = _____
5. fury + ous = _____
6. shine + y + est = _____
7. city + es = _____
8. noise + y + ly = _____
9. spot + y = _____
10. fury + ous + ly = _____

E Each sentence has one misspelled word. Write each word correctly on the blank.

1. The boxes were filled with brushs and watches. _____
2. That glorious day at prescool was the happiest day of her life. _____
3. Kim had been so thirsty that the sight of water made her joyus. _____

Lesson 35 is a test lesson. There is no worksheet.

Name _____ 36

A

1. do not = _____
2. we will = _____
3. were not = _____
4. let us = _____
5. here is = _____
6. are not = _____
7. they will = _____
8. they are = _____

B Fill in the blanks to show the morphographs in each word.

1. _____ + _____ + _____ = inspection
2. _____ + _____ + _____ = easiest
3. _____ + _____ = beautiful
4. _____ + _____ + _____ = container
5. _____ + _____ + _____ + _____ = exceptional
6. _____ + _____ + _____ = protection
7. _____ + _____ + _____ = relative
8. _____ + _____ + _____ = joyously
9. _____ + _____ + _____ = cloudiness
10. _____ + _____ + _____ = trials

C Each sentence has one misspelled word. Write each word correctly on the blank.

1. Did you preview the progect before you rejected it? _____
2. The first person who passes the goal claimes the prize. _____
3. She was too pasive to make plans about where to settle. _____

Lesson 36

D Write s or es in the second column.
Then add the morphographs together.

1. fly + _____ = _____

2. search + _____ = _____

3. union + _____ = _____

4. dress + _____ = _____

5. carry + _____ = _____

6. reach + _____ = _____

7. deny + _____ = _____

8. brush + _____ = _____

9. box + _____ = _____

10. play + _____ = _____

END OF LESSON 36

Name _____ 37

A

1. _____   4. _____
2. _____   5. _____
3. _____

B Make 8 real words from the morphographs in the box.

| ly | glory | nerve | ous | joy | study | vary |

1. _____   5. _____
2. _____   6. _____
3. _____   7. _____
4. _____   8. _____

C Write the contractions for the words below.

1. that is   = _____   5. they have = _____
2. we are   = _____   6. who is   = _____
3. should not = _____   7. can not   = _____
4. they will = _____   8. could not = _____

Lesson 37

D Add the morphographs together.

1. force + ful + ly = _____
2. friend + ly + ness = _____
3. in + tent + ion = _____
4. re + fuse + al = _____
5. dis + charge + ed = _____
6. story + es = _____
7. please + ure = _____
8. fury + ous + ly = _____
9. pro + gress + ive + ly = _____
10. dis + count + s = _____

E Each sentence has one misspelled word. Write each word correctly on the blank.

1. I have a famous relativ who has many riches. _____
2. An unexpected, poisonus gas presented a danger. _____
3. I take my time doing my taxes, exept when I'm expecting a refund. _____

END OF LESSON 37

Name _____

A

1. _____
   _____

2. _____
   _____

B

1. _____   4. _____
2. _____   5. _____
3. _____   6. _____

C Write the correct word for each sentence.

1. I poked a **hole/whole** in my worksheet.   _____
2. Would you care for a **peace/piece** of pie?   _____
3. Robin didn't **hear/here** the question.   _____
4. **Too/Two** police officers visited our school.   _____
5. Our house became **vary/very** warm.   _____
6. The dog's **tail/tale** is short.   _____
7. Please **right/write** me a letter.   _____
8. We went **to/too** see a play.   _____

Lesson 38

D Write s or es in the second column. Then add the morphographs together.

1. spray + _____ = _____
2. catch + _____ = _____
3. vary + _____ = _____
4. dry + _____ = _____
5. stretch + _____ = _____
6. hurry + _____ = _____
7. stay + _____ = _____
8. glass + _____ = _____

E Add the morphographs together.

1. dis + please + ing = _____
2. speed + y + est = _____
3. re + spect + ful = _____
4. danger + ous + ly = _____
5. in + crease + ing + ly = _____
6. please + ure = _____

END OF LESSON 38

Name _____

A

1. _____

2. _____

B

1. _____ 4. _____
2. _____ 5. _____
3. _____ 6. _____

C Write the correct spelling for each word.
Then write one of these letters after each number.

Write **O** if the word is spelled by just putting the morphographs together.
Write **A** if the final-**e** rule explains why the spelling is changed.
Write **B** if the doubling rule explains why the spelling is changed.
Write **C** if the **y**-to-**i** rule explains why the spelling is changed.

1. _____ place + ment = _____
2. _____ plan + ed = _____
3. _____ large + ly = _____
4. _____ deny + al = _____
5. _____ get + ing = _____
6. _____ worry + er = _____
7. _____ spot + less = _____
8. _____ rage + ing = _____
9. _____ dog + y = _____
10. _____ play + er = _____

Lesson 39

D. Circle the misspelled word in each group. Then write it correctly on the line.

1. feature
   ditch
   poisonus
   flying
   _____

2. hopeful
   blissful
   stopper
   sieze
   _____

3. portabel
   contain
   dislike
   trapped
   _____

4. ledge
   photograf
   shouldn't
   passage
   _____

5. rental
   worker
   preveiw
   actively
   _____

6. finest
   conserve
   perserve
   reserve
   _____

7. lightly
   catching
   hotest
   driest
   _____

8. hopefulnes
   thoughtful
   restlessness
   throughout
   _____

E. Each sentence has one misspelled word. Write each word correctly on the blank.

1. The crys of the babies stopped when they saw the toys.   _____
2. Everyone tries to be respectful of their unyon.   _____
3. The boys are picking beries near the river.   _____

Lesson 40 is a test lesson. There is no worksheet.

Name _____

A

ready   build   bought   simple   cross   chance

B

1. _____   4. _____
2. _____   5. _____
3. _____

C Write the contractions for the words below.

1. were not   = _____   5. are not   = _____
2. they will   = _____   6. did not   = _____
3. does not   = _____   7. they are = _____
4. I have   = _____   8. we have   = _____

D Draw a line from each word to its clue.

1. whole •   • I'm going to _____ a report.

2. hole   •   • something great

3. feat   •   • We dug a _____ in the ground.

4. right •   • also

5. write •   • all parts together

6. too   •   • My _____ are sore from jogging.

7. feet   •   • Don't turn left. Turn _____ .

Lesson 41   **65**

E Add the morphographs together.

1. state + ion = _____
2. vise + ion = _____
3. physic + al = _____
4. re + sent + ed = _____
5. spin + er = _____
6. heave + y = _____
7. re + quest + ing = _____
8. duty + es = _____
9. mis + shape + en = _____
10. fame + ous = _____
11. real + ly = _____
12. re + late + ion = _____

END OF LESSON 41

Name

A

chief   niece   brief   grief   thief

B

1. _____   4. _____

2. _____   5. _____

3. _____

C

Lesson 42

D Fill in the blanks to show the morphographs in each word.

1. _____ + _____ = expel
2. _____ + _____ + _____ = refusal
3. _____ + _____ = pleasure
4. _____ + _____ = chiefly
5. _____ + _____ + _____ = respectable
6. _____ + _____ + _____ + _____ = misconception
7. _____ + _____ + _____ = descriptive
8. _____ + _____ = statement
9. _____ + _____ = station
10. _____ + _____ + _____ = relative
11. _____ + _____ + _____ = reinstate
12. _____ + _____ + _____ = ripening

E Make 9 real words from the morphographs in the box.

| ed | cover | un | re | dis | solve |

1. _____
2. _____
3. _____
4. _____
5. _____
6. _____
7. _____
8. _____
9. _____

END OF LESSON 42

Name _____

A

The committee had high regard for honesty and courage.

_____

_____

B

1. _____   5. _____

2. _____   6. _____

3. _____   7. _____

4. _____   8. _____

C

**Write s or es in the second column.
Then add the morphographs together.**

1. stay + _____ = _____

2. story + _____ = _____

3. try + _____ = _____

4. reach + _____ = _____

5. cross + _____ = _____

6. city + _____ = _____

7. ditch + _____ = _____

8. deny + _____ = _____

Lesson 43

D These words are in the word search.
Circle 7 or more of the words.

fact	know	wrap
diet	chief	heroic
win	fly	detect
tin	niece	reject

```
k  t  n  k  n  o  w
f  r  i  d  c  w  r
d  a  e  n  h  i  a
k  i  c  j  i  n  p
n  d  e  t  e  c  t
f  l  y  t  f  c  y
h  e  r  o  i  c  t
```

E Fill in the blanks to show the morphographs in each word.

1. _____ + _____ + _____ = produced
2. _____ + _____ = repel
3. _____ + _____ = devise
4. _____ + _____ + _____ = revision
5. _____ + _____ + _____ = artistic
6. _____ + _____ + _____ = disrespect
7. _____ + _____ + _____ = protection

F Each sentence has one misspelled word.
Write each word correctly on the blank.

1. The work on the new bridge is ready for its fisical inspection. _____

2. Major cities are planning better highway developement. _____

3. Her refusal to read the sience book was questionable. _____

END OF LESSON 43

Name _____

A

___ ___m___m___ ___t___t___ ___ ___ ___ ___

___ ___a___ ___ ___ ___h___ ___e___ ___y ___

___ ___ ___o___u___ ___ ___ .

_____

_____

B

1. _____ 4. _____

2. _____ 5. _____

3. _____ 6. _____

C

**Cross out the misspelled words in these sentences.
Then write the words correctly above the crossed-out words.**

My sience teacher is vary intresting.

A reporter photografed the frigthened people.

His mother bougth a simpley beautyful dress.

There reasoning was'nt logical.

The reporter hired a detective for protecion.

Goverment should protect the rites of people.

Lesson 44

D Add the morphographs together.

1. create + ion = _____
2. style + ish + ly = _____
3. dis + solve + ing = _____
4. un + re + vise + ed = _____
5. type + ic + al = _____
6. re + cept + ion = _____
7. de + part + ure = _____
8. de + cept + ive = _____
9. mis + place + ed = _____
10. re + strict + ion = _____
11. beauty + ful + ly = _____
12. photo + graph + y = _____

E Each sentence has one misspelled word. Write each word correctly on the blank.

1. Who's that player who catchs so well?   _____
2. Long trials make the judge nervus.   _____
3. Our intention was to dissarm the intruder.   _____

Lesson 45 is a test lesson. There is no worksheet.

Name _____

A

___ ___m__t__ ___ ____

_____ ___ ___e___

___ __u_____.

_____

_____

B

1. _____   5. _____
2. _____   6. _____
3. _____   7. _____
4. _____   8. _____

C   Complete the sentences correctly with these words.

| right | too | to | tale | various | their | there | tail |

1. Martin's desk is often covered with _____ things.

2. Ellen always knows the _____ thing to say.

3. We used rags to make a _____ for her kite.

4. Ana had the _____ answers for all the questions.

5. Helen and Charles built _____ own bicycle.

6. Terry's _____ about pirates was _____ far-fetched for me.

7. I would like you _____ put the books over _____ .

Lesson 46   73

D Write the correct spelling for each word.
Then write one of these letters after each number.

Write **O** if the word is spelled by just putting the morphographs together.
Write **A** if the final-**e** rule explains why the spelling is changed.
Write **B** if the doubling rule explains why the spelling is changed.
Write **C** if the **y**-to-**i** rule explains why the spelling is changed.

1. _____ ready + ness = _____
2. _____ sad + ness = _____
3. _____ large + ly = _____
4. _____ style + ish = _____
5. _____ edge + ing = _____
6. _____ class + ic + al = _____
7. _____ type + ic + al = _____
8. _____ hope + ing = _____
9. _____ hop + ing = _____
10. _____ duty + es = _____
11. _____ force + ful = _____
12. _____ boy + ish = _____

E Each sentence has one misspelled word.
Write each word correctly on the blank.

1. You shouldn't wash your silk dreses. _____
2. Let's look over that ledje. _____
3. Today's displeasing temperature and clowdiness _____
   made everyone unhappy.

END OF LESSON 46

Name _____

47

A

1. _____
_____

2. _____
_____

B

1. _____ 4. _____
2. _____ 5. _____
3. _____

C

_____
_____
_____
_____
_____
_____
_____
_____
_____
_____
_____
_____

Lesson 47 **75**

D Fill in the blanks to show the morphographs in each word.

1. _____ + _____ + _____ = producing
2. _____ + _____ + _____ = stylishly
3. _____ + _____ = simplest
4. _____ + _____ + _____ = protective
5. _____ + _____ + _____ = relation
6. _____ + _____ + _____ = designer
7. _____ + _____ = resign
8. _____ + _____ = signal

END OF LESSON 47

Name _____

A

today   yesterday   tomorrow   afternoon   evening

B

Some explorers discovered treasure on a magic island.

_____

_____

C

1. _____   4. _____
2. _____   5. _____
3. _____

D **Add the morphographs together.**

1. create + ive   = _____

2. create + ion   = _____

3. re + create + ion   = _____

4. dis + courage   = _____

5. re + gard + less   = _____

6. niece + es   = _____

7. re + quest + ed   = _____

8. in + tense + ive + ly = _____

E These words are in the word search.
Circle 7 or more of the words.

doubt	loan	plot
quote	bone	madly
state	louder	nasty
moss	agree	went

```
d  p  m  q  u  e
m  o  l  o  a  n
a  q  o  o  s  a
d  o  u  b  t  s
l  o  d  o  a  t
y  w  e  n  t  y
a  g  r  e  e  e
```

F Each sentence has one misspelled word.
Write each word correctly on the blank.

1. Mom agreed that we'er getting new glasses today. _____
2. The tourists from various countries traveled joyusly together. _____
3. We can catch bugs and put them in this contaner. _____

END OF LESSON 48

Name _____ 49

A

__ o __ __ __ __ __ o r e __ __
__ __ s c o __ __ __ __ __ __ e a s __ __
__ __ __ __ g __ __ s __ __ __ __.

_____

_____

B

1. _____ 4. _____
2. _____ 5. _____
3. _____ 6. _____

C

_____
_____
_____
_____
_____
_____
_____
_____
_____
_____
_____

Lesson 49 79

D. Write the contractions for the words below.

1. they had = _____
2. we are = _____
3. it is = _____
4. do not = _____
5. what is = _____

6. you will = _____
7. are not = _____
8. they are = _____
9. we have = _____
10. she will = _____

E. Circle the misspelled word in each group. Then write it correctly on the line.

1.	breakable	2.	increase	3.	exchange	4.	honesty
	dowbt		changing		chance		tomorow
	pleasure		noisily		wreckage		inspect
	peaceful		taxs		sturdyness		product

_____   _____   _____   _____

F. Each sentence has one misspelled word. Write each word correctly on the blank.

1. I bought a very basik yet artistic house. _____
2. Sue had a brief chance to meet the comittee. _____
3. The chief gave us a grafic description of the incident. _____

Lesson 50 is a test lesson. There is no worksheet.

Name _____

A

_ _ _ _   _ _ _ _ _ _ e _ _

_ _ _ _ _ _ _ _ _   _ _ _ a s _ _ _

_ _   _   _ _ g _ _   _ s _ _ _ _ .

_____

_____

B

1. _____ 4. _____
2. _____ 5. _____
3. _____ 6. _____

C   Draw a line from each word to its clue.

1. sale • • The Smiths keep ▮▮▮ dog outside.

2. weather • • they are

3. their • • a part of something

4. there • • cold and cloudy

5. they're • • I'm going ▮▮▮ Dawn does or not.

6. whether • • lower prices

7. piece • • Tim has a ▮▮▮ in his knee.

8. pain • • The pencil sharpener is over ▮▮▮ .

Lesson 51 81

D Add the morphographs together.

1. trans + gress + ion = _____
2. pre + fer = _____
3. dis + courage + ment = _____
4. fine + ish + ed = _____
5. soft + en + ing = _____
6. con + quest + s = _____
7. in + flame + ed = _____
8. scare + y + est = _____
9. tribe + al = _____
10. clean + ly + ness = _____
11. stress + ful = _____
12. de + sign + er = _____

E Each sentence has one misspelled word. Write each word correctly on the blank.

1. The oil Ted discovered is thicker than tipical oil. _____
2. My neice is building a simple home. _____
3. He will look foolish if he dosen't revise this text. _____

END OF LESSON 51

Name _____   52

A

1. _____
   _____

2. _____
   _____

B

1. _____   4. _____
2. _____   5. _____
3. _____

C Fill in the circle marked R if the underlined word is spelled right.
Fill in the circle marked W if the underlined word is spelled wrong.

1. Their actions showed great <u>coorage</u>.   R   W
2. The <u>comittee</u> has made its decision.   R   W
3. Pauline is the <u>luckiest</u> person I know.   R   W
4. <u>Governments</u> are made up of people.   R   W
5. It is <u>to</u> warm outside to snow.   R   W
6. Running is good <u>exercise</u>.   R   W

Lesson 52

D Fill in the blanks to show the morphographs in each word.

1. _____ + _____ + _____ = realistic
2. _____ + _____ + _____ = translation
3. _____ + _____ + _____ = disgraceful
4. _____ + _____ + _____ = spherical
5. _____ + _____ + _____ = production
6. _____ + _____ + _____ = disrespect
7. _____ + _____ + _____ = prescription
8. _____ + _____ = texture
9. _____ + _____ + _____ = trickiest
10. _____ + _____ + _____ = furiously

E Circle each short word that ends in <u>cvc</u>.

Remember: The letters **y** and **w** are vowel letters at the end of a morphograph.
The letter **x** acts like two consonant letters.
Short words have 3 or 4 letters.

1. drop
2. flaw
3. plan
4. fix
5. trip
6. major
7. jar
8. pool
9. shop
10. danger
11. stray
12. spin

END OF LESSON 52

Name _____

A Fill in the circle marked R if the underlined word is spelled right.
Fill in the circle marked W if the underlined word is spelled wrong.

1. Anne's father goes to school in the <u>evning</u>. R W
2. Someone forgot to <u>clothes</u> the door. R W
3. Lisa's <u>honisty</u> always paid off. R W
4. I don't understand Bob's <u>edginess</u>. R W
5. We formed a <u>commitee</u> to plan the party. R W
6. Have you finished <u>writing</u> your report? R W

B

1. _____ 5. _____
2. _____ 6. _____
3. _____ 7. _____
4. _____ 8. _____

C Make 12 real words from the morphographs in the box.

| fer | scribe | trans | pre | port | con | de | re | serve |

1. _____ 7. _____
2. _____ 8. _____
3. _____ 9. _____
4. _____ 10. _____
5. _____ 11. _____
6. _____ 12. _____

Lesson 53 85

D Figure out the rules and write them.

cvc and the next . . . in a short word when the . . . double the final **c** . . . word ends . . . morphograph begins with **v**

_____

_____

and the next morphograph . . . to **i** in a word when the . . . change the **y** . . . word ends consonant-and-**y** . . . begins with anything except **i**

_____

_____

_____

E Fill in the blanks to show the morphographs in each word.

1. _____ + _____ + _____ = exception
2. _____ + _____ = expel
3. _____ + _____ + _____ = provision
4. _____ + _____ + _____ = transaction
5. _____ + _____ = dispel
6. _____ + _____ + _____ = container

END OF LESSON 53

Name _____ 54

A

tragic   comic   critic   medic   pulse

B

1. _____
   _____

2. _____
   _____

C

1. _____ 4. _____
2. _____ 5. _____
3. _____ 6. _____

D Write s or es in the second column. Then add the morphographs together.

1. loss + _____ = _____
2. tray + _____ = _____
3. puppy + _____ = _____
4. bench + _____ = _____
5. evening + _____ = _____
6. wish + _____ = _____
7. monkey + _____ = _____
8. body + _____ = _____

E Add the morphographs together.

1. dis + pose + al = _____
2. pro + duct + ion = _____
3. pro + vise + ion = _____
4. ready + ly = _____
5. critic + al = _____
6. type + ic + al = _____
7. ex + cept + ion + al = _____
8. fine + al + ly = _____
9. athlete + ic = _____
10. mis + in + form + ed = _____
11. peace + ful + ly = _____
12. photo + graph + y = _____

F Each sentence has one misspelled word. Write each word correctly on the blank.

1. Tom resented the simple revison that Bill made. _____
2. Unresolved greif doesn't go away. _____
3. I beleive I've misplaced two packages. _____

Lesson 55 is a test lesson. There is no worksheet.

88   Lesson 54

Name _____

A

show   blow   know   grow   throw   draw

B

1. _____   4. _____

2. _____   5. _____

3. _____

C

_____
_____
_____
_____
_____
_____
_____
_____

Lesson 56

D **Write the correct word for each sentence.**

1. Martin always hangs up his **close/clothes**. _____
2. I don't **know/no** the answer. _____
3. Our club **meats/meets** after school. _____
4. There is a **loan/lone** tree growing in our yard. _____
5. The tickets will be for **sail/sale** in the morning. _____
6. We can't **hear/here** the music. _____

E **Add the morphographs together.**

1. comic + al = _____
2. ex + pose + ure = _____
3. dis + courage + ment = _____
4. sculpt + ure = _____
5. trans + late + ed = _____
6. ex + press + ive = _____
7. pro + pose + al = _____
8. de + fine + ing = _____

F **Each sentence has one misspelled word. Write each word correctly on the blank.**

1. We searched trughout the state to discover a new star. _____
2. Her vision of the future dosen't seem foolish to me. _____
3. I was distracted and missplaced my contract. _____

END OF LESSON 56

Name _____ 57

A

1. _____ 5. _____
2. _____ 6. _____
3. _____ 7. _____
4. _____ 8. _____

B Fill in the blanks to show the morphographs in each word.

1. _____ + _____ + _____ = invention
2. _____ + _____ + _____ = disposal
3. _____ + _____ + _____ = appraisal
4. _____ + _____ + _____ = transaction
5. _____ + _____ + _____ + _____ = undiscovered
6. _____ + _____ = chancy
7. _____ + _____ + _____ = dangerously
8. _____ + _____ + _____ + _____ = increasingly

Lesson 57

C These words are in the word search. Circle 7 or more of the words.

blow	fill	athlete
team	often	city
loan	flaw	head
taxes	noun	produce

a	t	o	f	t	e	n
t	t	b	i	e	f	o
c	a	h	l	a	l	u
i	x	e	l	o	a	n
t	e	a	m	e	w	o
y	s	d	o	e	t	e
p	r	o	d	u	c	e

END OF LESSON 57

Name _____

58

A

rhythm   cycle   sphere

B

1. _____
   _____

2. _____
   _____

C

_____
_____
_____
_____
_____
_____
_____
_____

D

cause	island	provision	prevention
explore	questionable	describe	through
doubtful	frightening	exposure	increases

E Fill in the circle marked R if the underlined word is spelled right.
Fill in the circle marked W if the underlined word is spelled wrong.

1. Lee would like to be a television <u>critic</u>. R W
2. We can <u>apoint</u> three people to the committee. R W
3. Who remembered to <u>cloze</u> the door? R W
4. I enjoy history and <u>sciense</u>. R W
5. My parents <u>approve</u> of my hobbies. R W
6. Cora's mother went to a <u>convention</u> in Paris. R W
7. We can <u>dispoze</u> of old business quickly. R W
8. The Massons love <u>there</u> new house. R W

F Each sentence has one misspelled word.
Write each word correctly on the blank.

1. Requesting a text revision is tipical at this stage. _____
2. If we don't meet her demands, she'll resine. _____
3. We have the job of transporting an invaluble treasure. _____

There are no worksheets for Lesson 59 and Lesson 60.

Lesson 58

Name _____

A

merge   ground   sleep   shame   while

B

Two scientists and their assistants were in an automobile accident.

_____

_____

C

1. sew + en = _____
2. know + en = _____
3. ripe + en = _____
4. show + en = _____

5. prove + en = _____
6. grow + en = _____
7. throw + en = _____
8. gold + en = _____

D

Each sentence has one misspelled word. Write each word correctly on the blank.

1. The monkys became nervous and distracted by the end of the show. _____

2. His leg was inflamed after the tradgic accident. _____

3. She has a respectable job in the field of photoraphy. _____

E Add the morphographs together.

1. con + tent + s = _____
2. in + vent + ion = _____
3. re + verse + al = _____
4. ap + point + ment = _____
5. trans + fer = _____
6. rhythm + ic = _____
7. pro + pose + al = _____
8. in + tent + ion = _____
9. ex + pel = _____
10. sleep + less + ness = _____
11. rain + y + est = _____
12. hot + est = _____

F Draw a line from each word to its clue.

1. sew   • Jean's new _____ look nice.
2. clothes   • You should _____ to your grandmother.
3. right   • needle and thread
4. close   • All the countries signed a _____ treaty.
5. write   • Please _____ the window.
6. piece   • put seeds in the ground
7. sow   • not wrong
8. peace   • part of something

END OF LESSON 61

Name _____ 62

A

___ _ c i e _ _ _ s t _ ___
_ _ e i _ _ s _ _ s t a _ _ _ _ e _ _
_ _ _ _ _ u _ _ _ _ i l e
_ c c _ e _ _.

_____
_____

B

1. _____   5. _____
2. _____   6. _____
3. _____   7. _____
4. _____   8. _____

C

Add the morphographs together.
Remember to use the rule about adding en.

1. draw + en   = _____   5. loose + en = _____
2. strength + en = _____   6. threat + en = _____
3. blow + en   = _____   7. sew + en   = _____
4. know + en   = _____   8. grow + en   = _____

Lesson 62

D Make 18 real words from the morphographs in the box.

| ing | serve | tain | con | re | fine | form | de |

1. _____
2. _____
3. _____
4. _____
5. _____
6. _____
7. _____
8. _____
9. _____
10. _____
11. _____
12. _____
13. _____
14. _____
15. _____
16. _____
17. _____
18. _____

E Each sentence has one misspelled word. Write each word correctly on the blank.

1. She looked more boyish in athletic cloths. _____
2. She refussed to take a prescription drug for her treatment. _____
3. The last athlete finaly finished the race. _____

END OF LESSON 62

98 Lesson 62

Name _____

A

B

1. _____   5. _____
2. _____   6. _____
3. _____   7. _____
4. _____   8. _____

C   Fill in the blanks to show the morphographs in each word.

1. _____ + _____ + _____ = shamefully
2. _____ + _____ + _____ = extension
3. _____ + _____ + _____ = provision
4. _____ + _____ + _____ = prevention
5. _____ + _____ + _____ + _____ = intentional
6. _____ + _____ + _____ = disposable
7. _____ + _____ + _____ = disclosure
8. _____ + _____ = denial
9. _____ + _____ + _____ = rejection
10. _____ + _____ + _____ = description

Lesson 63

D Circle the misspelled word in each group. Then write it correctly on the line.

1. reqwest
   revision
   while
   feature
   _____

2. basic
   quoteable
   dangerous
   reverse
   _____

3. breifly
   physical
   spinning
   tomorrow
   _____

4. transfer
   photograph
   straight
   heavyest
   _____

5. science
   committee
   intrested
   duties
   _____

6. worried
   showen
   cloudiness
   pleasure
   _____

END OF LESSON 63

Name _____ 64

A

1. _____
   _____

2. _____
   _____

B

1. fer
2. vent
3. flat
4. blow
5. skid
6. tragic
7. pel
8. cap
9. win
10. draw
11. spirit
12. ject
13. grab
14. cover
15. spray
16. cut

C These words are in the word search. Circle 7 or more of the words.

shake   scope   thousand
athlete niece   equal
under   friend   voice
transact seed   farm

```
a  t  h  s  v  o  i  c  e
a  t  h  l  e  t  e  a  v
f  s  c  o  p  e  v  s  e
r  a  h  v  u  n  d  e  r
i  t  r  a  n  s  a  c  t
e  v  s  m  k  f  a  e  a
n  i  e  c  e  e  s  n  a
d  n  e  e  q  u  a  l  d
```

Lesson 64   101

D Add the morphographs together.
Remember to use your spelling rules.

1. rhythm + ic + al = _____
2. draw + en = _____
3. for + give + en = _____
4. un + in + tend + ed = _____
5. in + tent + ion + al = _____
6. grow + en = _____
7. shop + er = _____
8. vent + ure + ed = _____
9. ease + y + ly = _____
10. ex + pose + ure = _____

E Each sentence has one misspelled word.
Write each word correctly on the blank.

1. In photography, light exposeure is important, _____
   regardless of the time of day.
2. Let me show you how to make a beutiful glass _____
   sphere.
3. Mom is hurrying to finish sewing her formil gown. _____

Lesson 65 is a test lesson. There is no worksheet.

Name _____

A

1. _____
   _____
2. _____
   _____

B

1. _____   4. _____
2. _____   5. _____
3. _____   6. _____

C

Lesson 66

D

Write <u>s</u> or <u>es</u> in the second column.
Then add the morphographs together.

1. trophy + _____ = _____

2. fox + _____ = _____

3. lily + _____ = _____

4. ground + _____ = _____

5. peach + _____ = _____

6. pony + _____ = _____

7. crash + _____ = _____

8. monkey + _____ = _____

E

Fill in the blanks to show the morphographs in each word.

1. _____ + _____ + _____ + _____ = misinformed
2. _____ + _____ + _____ = carelessly
3. _____ + _____ + _____ = cheerfulness
4. _____ + _____ + _____ = instruction
5. _____ + _____ + _____ = reaction
6. _____ + _____ + _____ = descriptive
7. _____ + _____ + _____ = pretending
8. _____ + _____ + _____ = appointment
9. _____ + _____ + _____ = unbreakable
10. _____ + _____ + _____ = spherical
11. _____ + _____ = worthy
12. _____ + _____ + _____ = tightening

END OF LESSON 66

Name _____

A

1. _____
   _____

2. _____
   _____

B

1. _____   5. _____
2. _____   6. _____
3. _____   7. _____
4. _____   8. _____

C Choose two words from the list to complete each sentence.

| write | seen | scene | close | threw |
| vary | clothes | through | very | right |

1. Bonnie and Wayne found the _____ _____ for winter.

2. I have _____ many stars _____ my telescope.

3. I like to _____ the _____ that I'm painting.

4. The salesman _____ in a free trip to _____ the sale.

5. Jane has _____ Chan _____ his name in Chinese.

Lesson 67

D Add the morphographs together.

1. fail + ure = _____
2. trans + plant = _____
3. wake + en + ing = _____
4. con + struct + ion = _____
5. build + ing = _____
6. in + tent + ion = _____
7. re + tain + ed = _____
8. de + cept + ion = _____
9. sub + merge = _____
10. ex + cept + ion + al = _____
11. pro + tect + ive = _____
12. art + ist + ic = _____
13. trans + late + ed = _____
14. de + part + ure = _____

E Each sentence has one misspelled word. Write each word correctly on the blank.

1. How do you propose to design this mision? _____
2. The typist doesn't aprove of the content of the paper. _____
3. The commissioner was very criticle of the designer. _____

END OF LESSON 67

68

A

pound   habit   saint   brother   sister   false

B

1. _____   4. _____

2. _____   5. _____

3. _____   6. _____

C

_____
_____
_____
_____
_____
_____
_____
_____
_____

D Write the correct spelling for each word.
Then write one of these letters after each number.

Write **O** if the word is spelled by just putting the morphographs together.
Write **A** if the final-**e** rule explains why the spelling is changed.
Write **B** if the doubling rule explains why the spelling is changed.
Write **C** if the **y**-to-**i** rule explains why the spelling is changed.

1. _____ vary + ous = _____
2. _____ cycle + ist = _____
3. _____ get + ing = _____
4. _____ pay + ment = _____
5. _____ state + ment = _____
6. _____ type + ist = _____
7. _____ live + ly + ness = _____
8. _____ fury + ous = _____
9. _____ skin + ed = _____
10. _____ friend + ly + est = _____
11. _____ cube + ic = _____
12. _____ beauty + ful = _____

E Cross out the misspelled words in these sentences.
Then write the words correctly above the crossed-out words.

I wood like to toor a seenic iland.

He took a chanse when he crossed that old brige.

END OF LESSON 68

Name _____

A

1. _____
   _____

2. _____
   _____

B

1. _____   4. _____

2. _____   5. _____

3. _____   6. _____

C Make 9 real words from the morphographs in the box.

| tract | con | ject | in | ion | duct | re |

1. _____   6. _____

2. _____   7. _____

3. _____   8. _____

4. _____   9. _____

5. _____

Lesson 69   **109**

D Fill in the blanks to show the morphographs in each word.

1. _____ + _____ = falsely

2. _____ + _____ + _____ = insisted

3. _____ + _____ + _____ = subtraction

4. _____ + _____ + _____ + _____ = respectfully

5. _____ + _____ + _____ = reversal

6. _____ + _____ + _____ = recreation

7. _____ + _____ + _____ = resigned

8. _____ + _____ + _____ = objective

E Cross out the misspelled words in these sentences.
Then write the words correctly above the crossed-out words.

An unknowen athelete defeated the famus runner.

I have progresed wonderfully with my sciense project.

Lesson 70 is a test lesson. There is no worksheet.

Name _____

A

1. logic + ly = _____
2. proud + ly = _____
3. graph + ic + ly = _____
4. real + ly = _____
5. nice + ly = _____
6. athlete + ic + ly = _____

B

1. _____ 4. _____
2. _____ 5. _____
3. _____

C

cyclist	assistant	rhythm	accident
productive	proposal	extension	habit
around	structure	automobile	falsely

Lesson 71

D Add the morphographs together.

1. per + sist + ed = _____
2. dis + tract + ion = _____
3. a + wake + en = _____
4. pro + tect + ion = _____
5. ob + serve + ing = _____
6. ex + press + ion = _____
7. con + tent + ment = _____
8. un + ap + prove + ed = _____
9. storm + y + ness = _____
10. de + light + ful = _____

E Draw a line from each word to its clue.

1. sow   •   •   I forgot to ▭ the closet door.
2. scene   •   •   what you wear
3. close   •   •   The sun on the water made a beautiful ▭.
4. tail   •   •   also
5. clothes   •   •   Did you put those things ▭?
6. their   •   •   plant seeds
7. there   •   •   I think ▭ coming home soon.
8. they're   •   •   The dogs are scratching ▭ fleas.
9. too   •   •   Our cat doesn't have a ▭.

There is no worksheet for Lesson 72.

Name _____

A

That student appears to be thorough and conscientious.

_____

_____

B Add the morphographs together.
Remember the rule about adding al before ly.

1. critic + ly = _____
2. cost + ly = _____
3. hero + ic + ly = _____
4. magic + ly = _____
5. firm + ly = _____
6. rhythm + ic + ly = _____
7. chief + ly = _____
8. comic + ly = _____

C

1. _____ 4. _____
2. _____ 5. _____
3. _____ 6. _____

D Add the morphographs together.

1. per + fect + ion = _____
2. com + press + ion = _____
3. ob + serve + er = _____
4. a + ground = _____
5. re + sist + ed = _____
6. sub + merge + ed = _____
7. in + struct + ion + al = _____
8. per + form + er = _____
9. ob + long = _____
10. a + long = _____
11. ob + ject + ion = _____
12. sub + tract + ion = _____

E Each sentence has one misspelled word. Write each word correctly on the blank.

1. Please forgive me for forgetting my apointment. _____
2. The waves extended out in a rythmical pattern. _____
3. The automobile was defective and could cause an acident. _____
4. Can you easiley define the contents of the contract? _____

END OF LESSON 73

A

____ _____e__ __pea__ __ __ __orou__ ___ ____sc i__ t i___.

_____

_____

B

1. _____ 4. _____
2. _____ 5. _____
3. _____

C

1. _____

   _____

2. _____

   _____

D Add the morphographs together.
Remember to use the rule about adding al before ly.

1. strict + ly = _____

2. graph + ic + ly = _____

3. physic + ly = _____

4. round + ly = _____

5. critic + ly = _____

6. athlete + ic + ly = _____

7. like + ly = _____

8. danger + ous + ly = _____

E Circle the misspelled word in each group.
Then write it correctly on the line.

1. useless
   realy
   changing
   strength
   _____

2. sleepyness
   athletic
   furious
   basic
   _____

3. nineteen
   fashion
   version
   cheif
   _____

4. photograph
   vizion
   breathless
   spirit
   _____

5. sieze
   duties
   request
   settle
   _____

6. straight
   explain
   hopefully
   thrown
   _____

Lesson 75 is a test lesson. There is no worksheet.

Name _____

A

___ _____ _____ __

__ _____ ___

_____.

_____

_____

B

loaf   calf   half   shelf   wolf

C

_____
_____
_____
_____
_____
_____
_____
_____
_____

Lesson 76

D Fill in the blanks to show the morphographs in each word.

1. _____ + _____ = spiritual
2. _____ + _____ = recur
3. _____ + _____ = compile
4. _____ + _____ + _____ = perfection
5. _____ + _____ + _____ = awaken
6. _____ + _____ + _____ = performer
7. _____ + _____ = insist
8. _____ + _____ + _____ = contraction
9. _____ + _____ + _____ + _____ = objectionable
10. _____ + _____ + _____ = destructive
11. _____ + _____ + _____ = forgiven
12. _____ + _____ + _____ = exposure

E Each sentence has one misspelled word. Write each word correctly on the blank.

1. What a shame that the hottest days were also the dryest days! _____
2. The ponies were graceful and quik. _____
3. Any failur to perform will end your contract. _____

END OF LESSON 76

Name _____

A

    wife   life   self   knife   leaf

B

1. _____
   _____

2. _____
   _____

C   **Write the correct word for each sentence.**

1. Have you **scene/seen** Mercury or Venus?   _____
2. The sun is shining **threw/through** the window.   _____
3. Our friends will be **hear/here** soon.   _____
4. The students finished **their/they're** work.   _____
5. Turn **right/write** at the corner.   _____
6. I soaked my **feat/feet** after the race.   _____
7. She will **sail/sale** her boat on the river.   _____
8. Do you know how to **sew/sow** buttons?   _____

Lesson 77

D   **Add the morphographs together.**

1. child + hood = _____

2. habit + ual = _____

3. trans + miss + ion = _____

4. de + frost + ing = _____

5. re + create + ion = _____

6. com + miss + ion + er = _____

7. globe + al + ly = _____

8. de + script + ion = _____

9. false + hood = _____

10. a + piece = _____

11. sub + miss + ive = _____

12. per + fect + ion = _____

END OF LESSON 77

Name _____

78

A

1. thief _____
2. wife _____
3. loaf _____
4. wolf _____

B

1. _____
   _____

2. _____
   _____

C

1. _____   5. _____
2. _____   6. _____
3. _____   7. _____
4. _____   8. _____

D **Each sentence has one misspelled word. Write each word correctly on the blank.**

1. The instruction was confuseing because it wasn't worded logically.   _____

2. Foxes have a habbit of smelling the ground near their homes.   _____

3. What is the objetive of the instruction you are using?   _____

Lesson 78 **121**

E

These words are in the word search.
Circle 9 or more of the words.

government   graphic
thousand   heroic
sort   tend
danger   wonder
spend   cement
alike   ground
shine   voters

g	t	t	w	c	s	h	i	n	e
g	h	t	g	o	e	p	g	t	c
g	o	v	e	r	n	m	e	n	t
r	u	c	o	n	a	d	e	n	e
o	s	o	r	t	d	p	e	n	d
u	a	l	i	k	e	r	h	r	t
n	n	c	c	h	e	r	o	i	c
d	d	a	n	g	e	r	s	m	c

F

Write the contractions for the words below.

1. can not   = _____
2. does not   = _____
3. you are   = _____
4. they will = _____
5. they have = _____
6. could not = _____
7. she is   = _____
8. are not   = _____

END OF LESSON 78

Name _____

79

A

1. _____
   _____

2. _____
   _____

B

1. _____   5. _____
2. _____   6. _____
3. _____   7. _____
4. _____   8. _____

C

Fill in the circle marked R if the underlined word is spelled right.
Fill in the circle marked W if the underlined word is spelled wrong.

1. Can you <u>discribe</u> a rose?   R   W
2. We <u>finished</u> our work early.   R   W
3. Some rules have <u>exseptions</u>.   R   W
4. I like the <u>mournings</u> more than the afternoons.   R   W
5. <u>Ninteen</u> players made the team.   R   W
6. He bought a dog for <u>protection</u>.   R   W
7. We went to the park <u>instead</u> of the beach.   R   W
8. My father often works <u>threwout</u> the night.   R   W

Lesson 79   123

D Fill in the blanks to show the morphographs in each word.

1. _____ + _____ + _____ = likelihood
2. _____ + _____ + _____ = usually
3. _____ + _____ + _____ = commission
4. _____ + _____ = recur
5. _____ + _____ = transmit
6. _____ + _____ = across
7. _____ + _____ + _____ = submerged
8. _____ + _____ = alone
9. _____ + _____ + _____ = observer
10. _____ + _____ + _____ = disgraceful
11. _____ + _____ + _____ = imperfect
12. _____ + _____ = station

E Each sentence has one misspelled word. Write each word correctly on the blank.

1. You're likley to incur a costly fine. _____
2. The performer created a deliteful show. _____
3. The shopper nervousley asked the assistants for help. _____

Lesson 80 is a test lesson. There is no worksheet.

Name _____

A

1. loaf _____
2. shelf _____
3. thief _____
4. wife _____
5. knife _____
6. life _____

B

void   friend   mobile   temple   proper   please

C

1. _____ 4. _____
2. _____ 5. _____
3. _____

Lesson 81

D Make 9 real words from the morphographs in the box.

| ob | ed | ject | pro | ion | in | de |

1. _____
2. _____
3. _____
4. _____
5. _____
6. _____
7. _____
8. _____
9. _____

E Add the morphographs together.
Remember to use the rule about adding <u>al</u> before <u>ly</u> when the word ends with the letters <u>ic</u>.

1. short + ly = _____

2. hero + ic + ly = _____

3. class + ic + ly = _____

4. beauty + ful + ly = _____

5. ethic + ly = _____

6. strict + ly = _____

7. logic + ly = _____

8. rhythm + ic + ly = _____

END OF LESSON 81

Name

A

1. _____

2. _____

B

C Circle the short cvc morphographs.

1. grab   4. cur   7. mud   10. pel   13. run

2. mit   5. vent   8. fer   11. ship   14. blow

3. tray   6. habit   9. speak   12. magic   15. critic

D Add the morphographs together.

1. act + ive + ate = _____
2. ex + tract + ion = _____
3. a + void + able = _____
4. sign + ate + ure = _____
5. ob + struct + ion = _____
6. pro + tect + ion = _____
7. please + ure = _____
8. con + serve + ate + ion = _____
9. re + fuse + al = _____
10. ex + plore + er = _____
11. im + mobile = _____
12. in + form + ate + ive = _____

END OF LESSON 82

Name _____ 83

A Write the plural for each word.
Remember to say the plural word to yourself.

1. leaf _____
2. self _____
3. calf _____
4. knife _____
5. thief _____
6. elf _____

B

pure   temper   vast   tempt   image

C

1. _____   5. _____
2. _____   6. _____
3. _____   7. _____
4. _____   8. _____

D

honesty   drawn   conservation   critical
science   discourage   assistant   basically
treasure   awhile   usually   accident
thoroughly   bought   avoidable   throughout

Lesson 83   129

E Write the correct spelling for each word.
Then write one of these letters after each number.

Write **O** if the word is spelled by just putting the morphographs together.
Write **A** if the final-**e** rule explains why the spelling is changed.
Write **B** if the doubling rule explains why the spelling is changed.
Write **C** if the **y**-to-**i** rule explains why the spelling is changed.

1. _____ pure + ist = _____
2. _____ clean + ly + ness = _____
3. _____ skid + ed = _____
4. _____ vise + ual = _____
5. _____ salt + y + est = _____
6. _____ shine + ing = _____
7. _____ hurry + ing = _____
8. _____ speed + y + ly = _____
9. _____ grip + s = _____
10. _____ baby + es = _____

F Each sentence has one misspelled word.
Write each word correctly on the blank.

1. The student's notebook was tradgically submerged   _____
   in the lake.

2. A cold compres basically can help an infection.   _____

3. This oblong shape makes a perfect struture.   _____

There are no worksheets for Lesson 84 and Lesson 85.

Name _____ 86

A

Their approach to acquiring knowledge fascinates me.

_____

_____

B

1. _____   5. _____
2. _____   6. _____
3. _____   7. _____
4. _____   8. _____

C Circle the misspelled word in each group. Then write it correctly on the line.

1. winner
   veried
   searches
   rhythmically
   _____

2. soften
   should'nt
   reduction
   misplaced
   _____

3. invention
   weight
   graphicly
   interesting
   _____

4. trophys
   stepping
   restriction
   committee
   _____

5. cheif
   activate
   vision
   extent
   _____

6. translate
   stretchs
   falsehood
   delightful
   _____

7. scenic
   guiding
   lighten
   feetured
   _____

8. unknown
   prospective
   preformer
   maintain
   _____

Lesson 86   131

D Add the morphographs together.

1. de + vast + ate + ing = _____
2. medic + ate + ion = _____
3. friend + ly + est = _____
4. con + fuse + ion = _____
5. re + ply + ed = _____
6. pre + script + ion = _____
7. re + ap + pear = _____
8. case + ual = _____
9. comp + press + ion = _____
10. sub + miss + ion = _____
11. ob + serve + ate + ion = _____
12. in + form + ate + ive = _____

E Each sentence has one misspelled word. Write each word correctly on the blank.

1. His usualy composed wife was very discouraged. _____
2. Cut the loafes in half with that knife. _____
3. Motherhood requires contientous and often physical work. _____

END OF LESSON 86

Name _____ **87**

A

_ _ _ _ _   _ _ p _ o a _ _   _ _
_ c q _ _ _ _ _   _ _ _ w l e _ _ _
_ _ s c _ _ _ _ _   _ _ .

_____
_____

B

1. _____
   _____

2. _____
   _____

C

1. _____   4. _____
2. _____   5. _____
3. _____   6. _____

D   Each sentence has one misspelled word.
Write each word correctly on the blank.

1. The bare discovered some wild berries.   _____

2. My friend doesn't usually permitt me to use her skates.   _____

3. The commisioner obtained permission to reduce our taxes.   _____

Lesson 87   133

E Add the morphographs together.
Remember to use the rule about adding al before ly.

1. proper + ly = _____
2. base + ic + ly = _____
3. physic + ly = _____
4. order + ly = _____
5. hero + ic + ly = _____
6. un + like + ly = _____
7. comic + ly = _____

F Fill in the blanks to show the morphographs in each word.

1. _____ + _____ + _____ = belongs
2. _____ + _____ + _____ = designate
3. _____ + _____ + _____ = replied
4. _____ + _____ + _____ = confusing
5. _____ + _____ = transmit
6. _____ + _____ + _____ = avoiding
7. _____ + _____ + _____ = describing
8. _____ + _____ + _____ = invention
9. _____ + _____ + _____ + _____ = activation
10. _____ + _____ + _____ = likelihood
11. _____ + _____ + _____ = proposal
12. _____ + _____ + _____ = objective

END OF LESSON 87

Name _____

88

A

1. _____
   _____

2. _____
   _____

B

1. _____   5. _____
2. _____   6. _____
3. _____   7. _____
4. _____   8. _____

C

Dear Pat,

    Thank you vary much for the pet lizard you sent me. Wood you believe that the little fellow has begun snaping at people? My aunt was playing with him last nite. Suddenly the lizard jumped up and bit her write on the nose. Luckyly the bite wasn't bad.

    I'm sending you a photograf of the lizard sleeping with our cat. Those too have become like bruthers.

    Thanks again for the unuseual pet.

Your freind,

Chris

_____
_____
_____
_____
_____
_____
_____
_____

Lesson 88

D Write s or es in the second column.
Then add the morphographs together.

1. apply + _____ = _____

2. reach + _____ = _____

3. duty + _____ = _____

4. press + _____ = _____

5. speak + _____ = _____

6. match + _____ = _____

7. stay + _____ = _____

8. rich + _____ = _____

E Write the contractions for the words below.

1. they will = _____

2. who is = _____

3. can not = _____

4. we are = _____

5. they have = _____

6. would not = _____

END OF LESSON 88

A

The people in the picture are very busy.

The man by the sink is looking at the clock.

He has only an hour to finush washing the dishes.

The sink is only half full, so the man is runing more water.

The girl has a box in her hand. She is going to defrost the freezer.

She has already cleaned the shelves.

The boy on the right is wrapping a loaf of bread he made.

He cut some of the bread with a knife and ate it.

Everyone is being helpful.

B

Lesson 90 is a test lesson. There is no worksheet.

91 Name _____

A

1. _____
   _____

2. _____
   _____

B

1. _____   5. _____
2. _____   6. _____
3. _____   7. _____
4. _____   8. _____

C Circle the short cvc morphographs.

1. low   4. got   7. ply   10. get   13. cur
2. mit   5. bug   8. fox   11. pel   14. proper
3. temper   6. fer   9. stop   12. miss

D Make 12 real words from the morphographs in the box.

| struct | verse | in | con | tent | vent | ion |

1. _____   7. _____

2. _____   8. _____

3. _____   9. _____

4. _____   10. _____

5. _____   11. _____

6. _____   12. _____

END OF LESSON 91

Lesson 91 139

A

Adequately protecting the environment is a challenge.

_____

_____

B Add the morphographs together.

1. im + prove + ment = _____
2. e + value + ate = _____
3. be + lief + s = _____
4. ob + serve + ate + ion = _____
5. de + com + press + ion = _____
6. e + vent + ual = _____
7. con + vert + ed = _____
8. sign + ate + ure = _____

C Each sentence has one misspelled word. Write each word correctly on the blank.

1. Scientists proclame that the new medication will improve the condition. _____

2. The childhood belief in elves still fasinates many writers. _____

3. The endless search for my beautiful bracelet was depresing. _____

D Draw a line from each word to its clue.

1. bare • • what you wear
2. close • • not covered
3. bear • • Have you my gloves?
4. clothes • • I lost ▬ by exercising.
5. seen • • You must push the door hard to ▬ it.
6. scene • • Let's ▬ for the others before we leave.
7. wait • • an animal
8. weight • • The peaceful ▬ was interrupted by noisy campers.

E These words are in the word search. Circle 6 or more of the words.

today   draw   duty
tough   false agree
over   grief after
style

```
t  o  u  g  h  s
a  o  v  e  r  t
f  g  d  u  t  y
t  r  r  a  l  l
e  i  a  e  y  e
r  e  w  g  e  e
d  f  a  l  s  e
```

END OF LESSON 92

Lesson 92   141

93 Name _____

A

permit   rob   perform   spot   transfer   recur

B

_ _ e q _ a _ _ _ _   _ _ _ _ _ _ _ _ _
_ _   _ _ _ _ r o n _ _ _ _   _ _   _
_ _ _ _   l e n g _ _ .

C

1. _____   5. _____
2. _____   6. _____
3. _____   7. _____
4. _____   8. _____

142 Lesson 93

D Write the plural for each word.
Remember to say the plural word to yourself.

1. life _____
2. wolf _____
3. knife _____
4. thief _____
5. elf _____
6. leaf _____
7. half _____
8. shelf _____

E Fill in the blanks to show the morphographs in each word.

1. _____ + _____ + _____ = incurable
2. _____ + _____ + _____ = signature
3. _____ + _____ + _____ = perfection
4. _____ + _____ + _____ = disbelief
5. _____ + _____ + _____ = subtraction
6. _____ + _____ + _____ = improvement
7. _____ + _____ + _____ = textured
8. _____ + _____ + _____ = befriended
9. _____ + _____ + _____ = avoided
10. _____ + _____ + _____ + _____ = conversation
11. _____ + _____ + _____ = observer
12. _____ + _____ + _____ + _____ = transportation

END OF LESSON 93

Lesson 93   143

94

A

transmit   prefer   strain   hot

B

1. _____

2. _____

C

D Write the plural for each word.
Some of the words have <u>ves</u> in the plural. Some don't, so be careful.

1. wolf _____
2. cliff _____
3. chief _____
4. wife _____
5. gulf _____
6. roof _____
7. life _____
8. calf _____

E Choose one or more words from the list to complete each sentence.

| hole | write | week | whole | weak | right |

1. Jill visits her grandparents every month. Carlos visits his every _____ .

2. Jim ate the _____ pie, and now he is sick.

3. I must remember to _____ a thank-you letter to my aunt.

4. Next _____ is Kim's birthday party. Are you going?

5. Margot is only four years old, but she already knows how to read and _____ .

6. That beam is _____ because it has a _____ in it.

Lesson 95 is a test lesson. There is no worksheet.

Lesson 94

96 Name _____

A

commit   propel   reform   ship

B

END OF LESSON 96

Name _____ **97**

A

compel   stop   adjust   refer

B

1. _____   4. _____

2. _____   5. _____

3. _____   6. _____

C

Dear Customer:

    Are you spending more time than you need to on jobs arround the house? I am righting to inform you that we are now produsing the most usefull tool ever made for the home. The new E-Z Tool can do thousans of jobs in your home. It makes beds. It replases lightbulbs. It waters plants. It washs windows, serves your dinner, and cures bad breth, to. It comes packed in reuseable boxes. The E-Z Tool can easyly be put together using instrucshuns that come with each order.

    Please send us your order tomorow.

Sincerely,

I. M. Selling

_____

_____

_____

_____

_____

_____

_____

_____

_____

Lesson 97   **147**

D Fill in the blanks to show the morphographs in each word.

1. _____ + _____ = deceive

2. _____ + _____ + _____ = adjustment

3. _____ + _____ + _____ = emerged

4. _____ + _____ + _____ + _____ = observation

5. _____ + _____ + _____ = destruction

6. _____ + _____ + _____ = implied

E Each sentence has one misspelled word. Write each word correctly on the blank.

1. The robber avoided having a conversaion with the detective.   _____

2. Protecting the enviroment will save many lives.   _____

3. The king and his cheifs had an extended conversation.   _____

END OF LESSON 97

148   Lesson 97

Name

A

transmit　　　rerun　　　constrain　　　unstop

B

1. _____ + _____ + _____ = relentless

2. _____ + _____ + _____ = incomplete

3. _____ + _____ = surround

C

1. _____ + _____ + _____ = _____

2. _____ + _____ + _____ = _____

3. _____ + _____ + _____ = _____

4. _____ + _____ + _____ = _____

5. _____ + _____ + _____ = _____

6. _____ + _____ + _____ = _____

D Add the morphographs together.

1. e + duce + ate = _____
2. ad + vent + ure + ous = _____
3. con + temple + ate = _____
4. ad + miss + ion = _____
5. com + plete + ly = _____
6. de + vast + ate + ing = _____
7. con + sume + er = _____
8. sup + ply + es = _____
9. sur + face = _____
10. ad + dress = _____

E Write the plural for each word.
Some of the words have <u>ves</u> in the plural.
Some don't, so be careful.

1. photograph _____
2. cliff _____
3. leaf _____
4. shelf _____
5. calf _____
6. roof _____
7. wife _____
8. wolf _____

END OF LESSON 98

Name _____

99

A

repel   rob   subvert   outfit

B

1. _____
   _____

2. _____
   _____

C

1. _____ 4. _____

2. _____ 5. _____

3. _____ 6. _____

D

Each sentence has one misspelled word. Write each word correctly on the blank.

1. The rich and famous will pay any prise for fashion. _____

2. She started crying suddenley, but her tears couldn't be explained. _____

3. We through balls with the children to help them be more active. _____

Lesson 99   **151**

E Add the morphographs together.

1. re + late + ion + ship = _____
2. in + stant + ly = _____
3. sur + face = _____
4. sup + ply + es = _____
5. re + sume + ing = _____
6. ad + miss + ion = _____
7. e + vent + ful = _____
8. im + per + fect = _____
9. con + verse + ate + ion = _____
10. fright + en + ing = _____

F Cross out the misspelled words in these sentences.
Then write the words correctly above the crossed-out words.

The scientest was fasinated by his own invention.

Do we need perrmission to copy this report?

The new close I bougth do'nt fit very well.

The comittee on conservation is interested in preserving the enviroment.

Lesson 100 is a test lesson. There is no worksheet.

A

The champion became a prominent citizen.

_____

_____

B

END OF LESSON 101

102 Name _____

A

character   family   trouble   brought

B

___ _h___ i o_ __c_a__e
_ _____i_e__ c__i z e__.

C

1. _____   5. _____
2. _____   6. _____
3. _____   7. _____
4. _____   8. _____

D. Add the morphographs together.

1. de + tect + ion = _____
2. inter + view + ed = _____
3. pro + tect + ion = _____
4. re + act + ion = _____
5. in + vent + ion = _____
6. trans + gress + ion = _____
7. fact + ion + s = _____
8. con + tract + ion = _____
9. sup + pose + ed = _____
10. de + fect + ion = _____
11. vise + ion = _____
12. de + press + ion = _____

E. These words are in the word search. Circle 7 or more of the words.

supply	worth	style
court	rope	speak
out	believe	keeper
relate	state	soon

c	r	u	p	p	b	s
s	o	o	n	l	e	t
w	s	u	p	p	l	y
o	p	t	r	e	i	l
r	e	l	a	t	e	e
t	a	a	l	t	v	e
h	k	e	e	p	e	r

END OF LESSON 102

103 Name _____

A

		ion form?	**or** or **er** form?
1.	fact	_____	_____
2.	design	_____	_____
3.	invent	_____	_____
4.	act	_____	_____
5.	speak	_____	_____
6.	photograph	_____	_____

B

___ _____ o n ____ a __

_ _____ e __ _____ z e __ .

_____

_____

C

rob   repel   subvert   cut

156   Lesson 103

D   Circle the misspelled word in each group. Then write it correctly on the line.

1. character	2. pitiful	3. fashion	4. unknowen
replyed	worthless	thieves	basically
project	danjerous	resonable	brought
subtract	rhythm	magically	science

_____   _____   _____   _____

E   Circle the short cvc morphographs.

1. snap   3. mark   5. pel   7. critic   9. ceive

2. fer   4. ship   6. mit   8. cur   10. box

F   Add the morphographs together.

1. e + duce + ate = _____

2. inter + act + ion = _____

3. sup + press + ion = _____

4. e + mote + ion + al = _____

5. family + es = _____

6. trouble + ing = _____

END OF LESSON 103

104 Name _____

A

		ion form?	**or** or **er** form?
1.	transgress	_____	_____
2.	plant	_____	_____
3.	project	_____	_____
4.	compress	_____	_____
5.	retain	_____	_____
6.	tract	_____	_____

B

1. _____

2. _____

C Each sentence has one misspelled word. Write each word correctly on the blank.

1. Describing the robber's voise to the detective was a challenge. _____

2. The flawwed signature was a trick to deceive my assistant. _____

3. To adequeately evaluate the foxes, we will have to encourage observation. _____

Lesson 104

D Add the morphographs together.

1. rerun + ing = _____
2. refer + ing = _____
3. hot + est = _____
4. disarm + ed = _____
5. commit + ed = _____
6. ship + ing = _____
7. detect + ive = _____
8. snap + y = _____

E Make 12 real words from the morphographs in the box.

| ex | ion | com | press | re | sup | im | ive | de |

1. _____
2. _____
3. _____
4. _____
5. _____
6. _____
7. _____
8. _____
9. _____
10. _____
11. _____
12. _____

Lesson 105 is a test lesson. There is no worksheet.

A

1. _____   5. _____

2. _____   6. _____

3. _____   7. _____

4. _____   8. _____

B   Underline the morphograph that each word ends with. Then add the next morphograph.

1. admit + ed = _____

2. compel + ing = _____

3. expel + ed = _____

4. instruct + ive = _____

5. protect + ion = _____

6. big + est = _____

7. forgot + en = _____

8. recur + ing = _____

C

		ion form?	**or** or **er** form?
1.	dictate	_____	_____
2.	consume	_____	_____
3.	invent	_____	_____
4.	instruct	_____	_____
5.	stretch	_____	_____
6.	contract	_____	_____

D

1. _____ + _____ = profess
2. _____ + _____ = provide

E Fill in the blanks to show the morphographs in each word.

1. _____ + _____ + _____ = medication
2. _____ + _____ + _____ = prediction
3. _____ + _____ = promote
4. _____ + _____ + _____ + _____ = emotional
5. _____ + _____ + _____ = confession
6. _____ + _____ = traction
7. _____ + _____ + _____ = attractive
8. _____ + _____ = interview
9. _____ + _____ + _____ = intersection
10. _____ + _____ + _____ = instantly

F   **Each sentence has one misspelled word. Write each word correctly on the blank.**

1. The actor became emotional when he was interveiwed by a prominent photographer.   _____

2. To our disbelief, the supplies were shipped to a dishonist commissioner.   _____

3. The men avoided the vast cliffs because they were too much of a challange.   _____

END OF LESSON 106

Name _____

A

1. _____

2. _____

B Underline the morphograph that each word ends with. Then add the next morphograph.

1. repel + ing   = _____

2. remote + ly   = _____

3. submit + ing   = _____

4. commit + ment = _____

5. spot + less   = _____

6. prefer + ed   = _____

C

If there is an i-o-n form of the word, write it in the second column.
If there is no i-o-n form, leave the second column blank.
In the last column, write the word with the morphograph o-r or e-r.

		ion form?	**or** or **er** form?
1.	heavy	_____	_____
2.	vise	_____	_____
3.	invent	_____	_____
4.	misspell	_____	_____
5.	profess	_____	_____

D

1. _____ + _____ = inquire

2. _____ + _____ = resemble

E Complete each sentence correctly with one of these words.

| week | piece | desert | weight | weak |
| bare | bear | wait | peace | dessert |

1. Marty felt _____ all during his illness.

2. We go to school five days out of each _____ .

3. Fighters used to box with their _____ hands.

4. We will _____ for you after school.

5. A _____ of wood broke off the chair.

6. I would never _____ a friend in trouble.

7. When I eat too much _____ , I gain _____ .

There is no worksheet for Lesson 108.

109 Name

A

Several foreign nations considered the problem.

_____

_____

B

1. _____ 5. _____
2. _____ 6. _____
3. _____ 7. _____
4. _____ 8. _____

C

If there is an i-o-n form of the word, write it in the second column.
If there is no i-o-n form, leave the second column blank.
In the last column, write the word with the morphograph o-r or e-r.

		ion form?	or or er form?
1.	educate	_____	_____
2.	consume	_____	_____
3.	conduct	_____	_____
4.	invent	_____	_____
5.	write	_____	_____
6.	act	_____	_____

Lesson 109

D

Write the correct spelling for each word.
Then write one of these letters after each number.

Write **O** if the word is spelled by just putting the morphographs together.
Write **A** if the final-**e** rule explains why the spelling is changed.
Write **B** if the doubling rule explains why the spelling is changed.
Write **C** if the **y**-to-**i** rule explains why the spelling is changed.

1. _____ re + ply + ed = _____
2. _____ con + fuse + ion = _____
3. _____ chance + y = _____
4. _____ worth + y + ness = _____
5. _____ grip + ed = _____
6. _____ for + give + en = _____
7. _____ study + ing = _____
8. _____ storm + y + est = _____
9. _____ re + serve + ate + ion = _____
10. _____ shop + er = _____
11. _____ un + hurry + ed = _____
12. _____ settle + ment = _____

E

Circle the misspelled word in each group.
Then write it correctly on the line.

1. copying
   approve
   beleive
   forgot

2. medical
   perscription
   maddest
   immobile

3. were'nt
   puppies
   source
   remark

4. unhappy
   delightful
   famous
   tomorow

_____ _____ _____ _____

Lesson 110 is a test lesson. There is no worksheet.

A

_ _ _ e _ _ _   _ _ e i g _   _ _ _ _ _ _
_ _ s _ _ _ _ _ _ _ _ _   _ _ _   _ _ _ _ _ e _ .

B

1. _____

2. _____

C

Dear Terry,   April 1

    Last weak my famly went to visit relutives. We had a wonderful time.

    I had my photograph taken with a fameous scientest. My cousin and I dug a whole in the woods and found a hiden treasure. Now we are vary rich. Someone gave my sister a valueable automobile. Later we won a radio contest. The prize was a trip arround the world. On the way home, we caught a theif who was robing a store.

    April Fool's Day!

Sincerely,

Robin

D
Underline the morphograph that each word ends with. Then add the next morphograph.

1. compel + ing = _____
2. commit + ment = _____
3. report + er = _____
4. permit + ed = _____
5. prefer + ed = _____
6. recap + ing = _____
7. predict + ion = _____
8. recur + ing = _____

E Fill in the blanks to show the morphographs in each word.

1. _____ + _____ + _____ = confession
2. _____ + _____ + _____ = designer
3. _____ + _____ + _____ + _____ = resignation
4. _____ + _____ + _____ = promotion
5. _____ + _____ + _____ = divided
6. _____ + _____ + _____ = attractive
7. _____ + _____ + _____ + _____ = information
8. _____ + _____ + _____ = adventure

END OF LESSON 111

Name _____

A

1. _____
   _____

2. _____
   _____

B

1. _____   4. _____

2. _____   5. _____

3. _____

C

Lesson 112

D If there is an i-o-n form of the word, write it in the second column.
If there is no i-o-n form, leave the second column blank.
In the last column, write the word with the morphograph o-r or e-r.

		ion form?	or or er form?
1.	interview		
2.	instruct		
3.	contract		
4.	receive		
5.	invent		
6.	inspect		

E Make 8 real words from the morphographs in the box.

| verse | con | sign | re | serve | ion | ate |

1. _____   5. _____

2. _____   6. _____

3. _____   7. _____

4. _____   8. _____

END OF LESSON 112

Name _____

113

A

1. _____ 5. _____
2. _____ 6. _____
3. _____ 7. _____
4. _____ 8. _____

B

bound   prime   custom   legend   cave   grave   ready   scarce

C

END OF LESSON 113

Lesson 113   173

114 Name _____

A

1. _____

2. _____

B

1. _____ 4. _____

2. _____ 5. _____

3. _____

C Underline the morphograph that each word ends with. Then add the next morphograph.

1. permit + ed   = _____

2. unstop + able = _____

3. spin + ing   = _____

4. recur + ed   = _____

5. propel + er   = _____

6. invent + ive = _____

Lesson 114

D. Add the morphographs together.

1. re + quire + ment + s = _____
2. in + di + vide + ual = _____
3. de + cise + ion + s = _____
4. pro + fess + ion + al = _____
5. tempt + ate + ion = _____
6. at + tent + ion = _____
7. re + mote + ly = _____
8. mote + ive + ate = _____
9. di + strict = _____
10. un + sur + pass + ed = _____

E. Fill in the circle marked R if the underlined word is spelled right. Fill in the circle marked W if the underlined word is spelled wrong.

1. We ate fresh fruit for <u>desert</u>. Ⓡ Ⓦ
2. The study of insects <u>fascinates</u> me. Ⓡ Ⓦ
3. Jake's mother works for the <u>goverment</u>. Ⓡ Ⓦ
4. Our friends <u>bougth</u> a new automobile. Ⓡ Ⓦ
5. Some forms of energy are <u>destructive</u> to the environment. Ⓡ Ⓦ
6. My doctor won't write a <u>persription</u> unless it is really necessary. Ⓡ Ⓦ

Lesson 115 is a test lesson. There is no worksheet.

116 Name _____

A

It's probably not necessary to continue the competition.

_____

_____

B

1. _____   5. _____
2. _____   6. _____
3. _____   7. _____
4. _____   8. _____

C

If there is an **i-o-n** form of the word, write it in the second column.
If there is no **i-o-n** form, leave the second column blank.
In the last column, write the word with the morphograph **o-r** or **e-r**.

		ion form?	**or** or **er** form?
1.	vise	_____	_____
2.	profess	_____	_____
3.	review	_____	_____
4.	contract	_____	_____
5.	perform	_____	_____
6.	protect	_____	_____

D Add the morphographs together.
Remember to use your rule about adding <u>en</u>.

1. know + en = _____

2. tough + en = _____

3. draw + en = _____

4. sew + en = _____

5. grow + en = _____

6. prove + en = _____

E Fill in the blanks to show the morphographs in each word.

1. _____ + _____ + _____ = precisely

2. _____ + _____ = require

3. _____ + _____ + _____ = inquiry

4. _____ + _____ + _____ = commotion

5. _____ + _____ + _____ = remoteness

6. _____ + _____ + _____ = attraction

7. _____ + _____ + _____ + _____ = relationship

8. _____ + _____ + _____ = supplied

END OF LESSON 116

117 Name _____

A

___ ___ ___ ___ , ___ ___ ___ b a b ___ ___ ___ ___
___ ___ c ___ s s a ___ ___ ___ ___ ___ ___ ___ ___ ___ u e
___ ___ ___ ___ ___ ___ ___ e ___ ___ t ___ ___ .

_____

_____

B

1. _____

_____

2. _____

_____

C Add the morphographs together.

1. pro + fess + ion + al   = _____
2. di + stress + ing   = _____
3. re + sume + ed   = _____
4. ex + plore + ate + ion   = _____
5. dis + courage + ment   = _____
6. dis + sect   = _____
7. con + front + ate + ion = _____
8. im + proper + ly   = _____

D Draw a line from each word to its clue.

1. dessert • • My parents were ▓ in a small town.
2. barely • • The tourists had a ▓ view of the mountain.
3. married • • We ▓ finished the assignment.
4. weight • • Have you ▓ the new invention?
5. scenic • • something you eat
6. desert • • We changed our ▓ after school.
7. seen • • Pat lost ▓ by exercising.
8. clothes • • to leave

E Add the morphographs together.
Remember to use the rule about adding **al** before **ly**.

1. critic + ly = _____
2. graph + ic + ly = _____
3. de + light + ful + ly = _____
4. physic + ly = _____
5. real + ly = _____
6. base + ic + ly = _____
7. comic + ly = _____
8. un + like + ly = _____

END OF LESSON 117

118 Name _____

A

1. _____
   _____

2. _____
   _____

B

1. _____   4. _____
2. _____   5. _____
3. _____

C

1. _____ + _____ = record
2. _____ + _____ + _____ = dictionary

D Each sentence has one misspelled word. Write each word correctly on the blank.

1. To the relief of the students, the strict professer was dismissed. _____

2. Sevral nations provide protection to foreign citizens. _____

3. The gradual increase in temperature this week improoved everyone's mood. _____

4. The photographs of the island were remarkable. _____

E Write the plural for each word.

1. worry = _____
2. thief = _____
3. scratch = _____
4. chief = _____
5. wife = _____
6. bush = _____
7. study = _____
8. leaf = _____
9. view = _____
10. copy = _____

F Underline the morphograph that each word ends with. Then add the next morphograph.

1. forget + ing = _____
2. compel + ed = _____
3. inspect + ion = _____
4. dog + y = _____
5. transfer + ed = _____
6. contain + er = _____

END OF LESSON 118

119 Name _____

A

B Circle the short <u>cvc</u> morphographs.

1. water
2. fer
3. rent
4. poison
5. big
6. spirit
7. stay
8. cur
9. motor
10. pel
11. critic
12. box
13. mit
14. wander
15. low
16. flat

C Fill in the blanks to show the morphographs in each word.

1. _____ + _____ + _____ = dictionary
2. _____ + _____ + _____ + _____ = unrecorded
3. _____ + _____ + _____ = partially
4. _____ + _____ + _____ = precisely
5. _____ + _____ = married
6. _____ + _____ + _____ + _____ = preservation

D Each sentence has one misspelled word. Write each word correctly on the blank.

1. The reportor instantly knew that the information would be scarce.   _____

2. We permited the writer to use her notes.   _____

3. According to an old ledgand, the cave was the home of a frightening animal.   _____

Lesson 120 is a test lesson. This is the last worksheet in Grade 4.

Lesson 119   **183**

Word List

WORD   **LESSON**

Word	Lesson	Word	Lesson	Word	Lesson	Word	Lesson
accident	61	appear	78	awaken	71	boats	19
acquire	94	appears	73	awhile	83	bodies	54
acquiring	86	applied	87	babies	32	bone	48
across	79	applies	88	baby	96	book	101
action	23	apply	86	bare	83	bought	41
actions	52	appoint	56	barely	117	bound	113
activate	82	appointment	61	barred	17	box	89
activation	87	appraisal	57	base	4	boxes	27
active	23	appraise	56	basic	43	boxing	27
actively	33	approach	86	basically	71	boy	23
actor	103	approval	67	batch	36	boyhood	77
addictive	104	approve	56	be	19	boyish	46
address	98	aren't	36	bear	77	boys	31
adequate	108	around	71	beautiful	34	break	12
adequately	92	art	8	beautifully	44	breakable	3
adjust	94	artist	39	beauty	34	breath	7
adjusted	97	artistic	43	became	101	breathe	3
adjustment	96	artists	91	because	87	breathless	11
admission	98	assistant	67	befriended	93	bridge	12
admit	94	assistants	61	behave	86	brief	42
admitted	106	ate	18	behaved	93	briefly	63
adventure	98	athlete	17	belief	91	brightness	6
adventurous	98	athletes	7	beliefs	92	brother	9
advise	94	athletic	54	believable	94	brotherhood	84
after	92	athletically	71	believe	54	brotherly	69
afternoon	48	attain	104	belong	86	brothers	88
agree	21	attainment	108	belongs	87	brought	102
agreement	73	attempt	114	benches	54	brown	3
aground	73	attention	114	berries	32	brushes	26
alike	71	attest	104	beside	86	build	41
all	27	attract	104	best	9	building	42
alone	79	attraction	116	big	9	bushes	118
along	73	attractive	106	biggest	12	but	88
any	66	automobile	61	black	33	buzzes	26
anybody	19	avoidable	82	blow	56	cage	33
apart	71	avoided	93	blowing	96	cake	107
apiece	77	avoiding	87	blown	62	calf	76

184   Word List

WORD / LESSON

WORD	LESSON	WORD	LESSON	WORD	LESSON	WORD	LESSON
calves	78	classically	72	conduction	109	contracted	77
can	74	cleaned	89	conductor	109	contraction	76
can't	37	cleanliness	51	confer	51	contractor	106
carelessly	66	cliffs	94	confession	106	convent	91
carried	17	close	48	confine	19	convention	57
carries	32	closed	67	confinement	23	conversation	93
carry	84	clothes	46	conform	19	converse	91
carrying	17	cloudiness	36	confrontation	117	conversion	91
casual	86	coach	38	confronted	19	convert	88
catches	38	comic	54	confuse	82	converted	92
cause	22	comical	56	confused	88	coolest	11
cave	113	comically	73	confusing	83	copies	31
cement	78	commission	77	confusion	84	copying	19
challenge	92	commissioner	77	conjecture	27	costly	73
challenged	99	commit	78	conquests	51	couldn't	37
challenging	112	commitment	107	conscientious	73	count	34
champion	101	committed	96	conservation	82	courage	43
chance	41	committee	43	conserve	19	court	102
chancy	57	commotion	116	consider	113	courtship	97
change	16	compel	97	considered	109	cover	3
changing	23	compelled	118	consist	68	covered	42
character	102	compelling	97	constant	99	coverless	3
cheerful	6	competition	116	constrained	98	crashes	66
cheerfulness	66	compile	76	construct	64	crease	16
chew	22	complain	73	construction	66	creased	16
chief	42	completely	98	consume	97	create	17
chiefly	42	comply	86	consumer	98	creation	44
chiefs	94	compose	73	contain	1	creative	48
childhood	77	composer	103	container	36	cries	33
childish	44	composure	81	contemplate	98	critic	54
choice	38	compress	73	contempt	87	critical	54
choicest	12	compression	73	contend	62	critically	71
cities	34	compressor	104	content	59	cross	41
citizen	101	conceive	94	contention	91	crosses	43
claim	16	concept	24	contentment	71	crutch	38
claims	28	conception	41	contents	61	cry	13
clapping	24	concise	108	contest	104	crying	22
class	37	concur	74	context	23	cubic	68
classic	72	conduct	47	continue	116	cubically	71
classical	46	conducted	46	contract	67	curable	7

Word List

WORD		LESSON

Word	Lesson
cure	3
custom	113
cut	89
cutting	103
cycle	58
cyclist	68
damage	89
danger	28
dangerous	29
dangerously	38
darken	17
darker	13
darkest	11
deceive	94
deception	31
deceptive	24
decision	52
decisions	114
decisive	108
decompression	92
deduce	43
defeated	26
defection	102
defective	72
defector	104
defer	51
define	62
defining	17
deform	62
deforming	24
defrost	89
defrosting	77
defuse	82
dejected	27
delight	16
delightful	71
delightfully	117
delights	19
demote	103
denial	22

Word	Lesson
denies	36
deny	84
departed	18
departure	36
deport	16
depose	54
depress	19
depressing	92
depression	26
describe	16
describing	87
description	63
descriptive	42
desert	99
deserve	53
design	53
designate	82
designer	47
dessert	103
destruction	64
destructive	76
detain	33
detect	26
detecting	24
detection	28
detective	26
detectives	64
devastating	86
development	31
devise	41
dictate	104
dictation	106
dictator	106
diction	103
dictionary	118
didn't	41
diet	43
disarm	37
disarmed	104
disbelief	93

Word	Lesson
discharged	37
disclosure	63
discounts	37
discourage	48
discouragement	51
discover	42
discovered	42
discovering	39
disease	37
disgraceful	52
dishes	28
dishonest	58
dishonesty	54
dislike	37
dismiss	77
disorder	53
dispel	39
displeased	82
displeasing	38
disposable	63
disposal	54
dispose	54
disrespect	43
dissect	102
dissolve	42
dissolved	42
dissolving	44
distance	117
distant	107
distraction	71
distressing	117
district	114
ditch	37
ditches	43
divide	107
divided	111
division	107
doesn't	41
doggy	39
don't	36

Word	Lesson
doubt	2
doubtful	2
doubting	7
doubtless	2
draw	22
drawn	61
dress	34
dresses	36
dries	38
driest	76
drip	8
drop	52
dropper	14
drying	18
duties	2
duty	28
easiest	36
easily	64
easy	23
edginess	34
edging	46
edgy	23
educate	98
education	109
educator	109
eight	18
eject	92
elephant	113
elves	81
emerge	92
emerged	97
emotion	103
emotional	103
endless	1
environment	92
equal	64
ethically	81
evaluate	92
evening	48
evenings	54

Word List

WORD		LESSON

Word	Lesson
event	92
eventful	99
eventual	92
ever	82
except	26
exception	28
exceptional	36
exceptions	79
exchange	21
exchanging	21
exclaim	24
exercise	19
exercised	7
exercises	87
expel	39
expelled	106
explain	21
explained	32
exploration	108
explore	59
explorer	82
explorers	48
expose	54
exposed	58
exposure	56
express	21
expressed	26
expression	27
expressive	56
extend	62
extended	63
extension	63
extent	59
extract	67
extraction	71
facial	118
facing	21
fact	32
faction	103
factions	102
factor	103
factual	76
failure	67
fair	7
fairness	8
faithful	7
false	68
falsehood	77
falsely	69
families	103
family	102
famous	27
fanciest	18
farm	64
farmer	13
fascinate	91
fascinated	99
fascinates	86
fascinating	94
fashion	7
fashionable	8
fault	3
fearful	7
feat	9
feature	24
featured	39
features	33
featuring	29
feet	9
fence	4
final	13
finally	19
finely	17
fineness	17
finer	13
finest	17
finish	53
finished	51
firm	14
firmly	73
firmness	7
fitness	26
flat	32
flatly	14
flatness	13
flattest	66
flaw	23
flawed	26
flies	32
flop	34
fly	14
foolish	44
forbid	63
force	36
forceful	46
forcefully	37
foreign	109
forget	63
forgetful	68
forgetting	118
forgive	63
forgiven	64
forgiving	66
forgotten	106
fork	33
form	101
formal	12
formally	18
found	21
foxes	66
fresh	3
fresher	13
friend	64
friendliest	68
friendliness	31
friendly	53
friendship	97
fright	11
frighten	36
frightened	44
frightening	19
frost	14
fur	34
furious	27
furiously	34
furry	31
fury	28
fuss	36
getting	39
glass	38
glasses	38
global	13
globally	77
globe	9
glorious	28
gloriously	37
going	111
golden	61
govern	17
government	22
governments	52
grab	8
gradual	76
graphic	43
graphically	71
grave	113
great	18
greatest	11
greatness	59
grief	42
gripped	109
grips	83
ground	61
grounds	66
grow	56
grown	61
guide	4
guided	8
guiding	6
gulfs	94

Word List

WORD			LESSON
habit 68	hop 9	inflamed 51	intersection 106
habitual 77	hope 4	information 111	interview 101
had 114	hoped 18	informative 82	interviewed 102
half 76	hopeful 11	informed 19	interviewer 112
halves 78	hopefulness 39	informer 18	invaluable 26
handle 1	hopeless 6	inhuman 18	invent 57
handleless 1	hoping 6	injected 29	invented 58
hang 113	hopping 11	injection 27	invention 57
happiest 22	hottest 39	inland 18	inventive 72
happily 29	hour 89	inquire 107	inventor 103
happiness 17	house 12	inquiry 116	inverse 91
happy 13	hurried 21	insect 102	inversion 91
hardship 97	hurries 38	insects 106	invert 88
hardships 113	hurry 66	insist 68	inverted 93
harmless 77	hurrying 57	insisted 69	island 48
have 82	image 83	inspect 34	its 52
haven't 66	immobile 82	inspection 34	it's 49
having 9	immovable 99	inspector 112	I've 41
healthy 19	impart 87	instance 117	jacket 96
hear 8	imperfect 79	instant 99	jar 52
heavier 107	implied 97	instantly 99	joy 13
heaviest 63	imply 86	instead 19	joyous 27
heavy 41	import 87	instruct 64	joyously 36
hedge 34	imported 94	instruction 66	joys 31
helped 8	improperly 94	instructional 73	judge 12
helper 13	improve 87	instructions 97	keeper 102
helpful 89	improved 93	instructive 106	kick 36
helpless 1	improvement 88	instructor 103	kind 9
helplessly 19	inborn 18	intend 62	kindest 44
helplessness 6	incision 108	intensive 51	kindly 44
here 8	incomplete 98	intensively 48	kindness 6
here's 36	increase 19	intent 91	kings 21
heroic 43	increases 47	intention 37	knife 77
heroically 73	increasing 21	intentional 63	knives 81
hidden 111	increasingly 38	interaction 103	know 43
hiding 16	incur 74	intercept 101	knowledge 86
high 43	incurable 93	interested 13	known 61
hike 113	individual 114	interesting 39	large 34
hole 8	infect 72	intermission 101	largely 39
honesty 43	infection 74	intersect 102	largest 16

Word List

WORD			LESSON
last 4	lodge 38	meat 18	motherhood 77
latch 33	logic 4	medic 54	mothering 12
lately 24	logically 71	medical 73	motherless 2
leaf 77	lone 8	medicate 82	motivate 114
learn 86	loneliest 34	medication 86	motive 103
leave 4	lonely 16	meet 18	move 3
leaves 78	look 37	meets 56	movement 26
ledge 37	looking 89	merge 61	mud 96
legend 113	loose 11	merged 69	my 77
length 4	loosely 17	merry 112	name 4
lengthen 18	loosen 16	misconception 28	named 8
let's 36	lose 3	misfile 2	nastier 22
life 77	losses 54	misfiles 11	nastiest 18
lifeless 13	louder 31	mishandle 1	nasty 13
light 18	low 22	misinformed 54	nations 109
lighten 46	lower 26	misjudge 1	necessary 116
lighter 13	lowest 23	mismatch 1	nervous 37
lightest 46	luckiest 52	misplace 2	nervously 37
lightly 46	luckily 36	misplaced 44	nice 34
lights 21	lucky 21	misprint 1	nicely 71
likable 6	mad 9	misquote 4	niece 42
like 3	madder 17	misreported 19	nieces 48
liked 9	maddest 17	misshape 4	night 88
likelihood 77	made 52	misshapen 41	nineteen 7
likely 74	madly 17	mission 67	noisily 34
likeness 6	madness 14	misspell 3	note 4
likes 11	magic 47	misspeller 107	notion 26
lilies 66	magically 71	misspelling 8	object 67
line 101	main 107	mist 1	objection 73
listen 4	maintain 33	mistake 67	objectionable 76
listening 89	major 2	mistaken 36	objective 69
little 4	making 52	misuse 2	oblong 73
live 12	many 3	mobile 81	observation 86
livelihood 87	married 117	monkeys 54	observe 67
liveliness 68	marry 108	moon 89	observer 72
lives 79	massive 23	morning 7	observing 71
loaf 76	match 1	mornings 79	obstruction 82
loan 8	matches 26	moss 48	obtain 67
loaves 79	matchless 1	most 54	obtained 68
lock 89	maybe 4	mother 2	often 87

Word List **189**

Word List

WORD			LESSON
opposed 98	photo 32	pound 32	product 46
order 34	photograph 13	power 1	production 51
orderly 87	photographed 44	powerful 2	productive 48
our 91	photographer 103	powerfully 59	profess 106
out 102	photographs 98	powerless 2	profession 107
outfitted 99	photography 44	precise 108	professional 114
over 92	physical 1	precisely 116	professor 107
package 18	physically 74	predict 104	profile 22
pain 51	piece 8	prediction 106	profound 22
painful 2	pinches 33	prefer 51	profoundly 26
painfulness 6	pitiful 16	preferred 94	progress 24
park 34	pity 14	preschool 26	progressed 24
part 14	pitying 16	prescribe 53	progression 26
partial 118	place 2	prescription 52	progressive 28
partially 119	placed 12	preservation 119	progressively 37
passes 26	placement 39	preserve 26	project 27
passion 4	placing 12	press 16	projecting 31
passive 23	plan 8	presses 27	projection 33
patch 36	planned 11	pressure 24	projector 104
pay 24	plans 54	presume 97	projects 69
payment 68	planter 104	pretend 62	prolong 36
peace 8	play 13	pretended 64	prominent 101
peaceful 16	player 39	pretending 66	promote 103
peacefully 54	playful 16	prevent 57	promoted 114
peaches 66	playing 16	prevention 59	promoter 106
people 13	plays 31	preview 26	promotion 109
perceive 94	please 26	price 2	propel 39
perception 69	pleasure 31	priceless 6	propeller 96
perceptive 74	pledge 37	pricing 8	proper 81
perfect 72	plot 48	prime 113	properly 84
perfection 73	point 119	print 2	proposal 56
perfectly 98	pointless 1	printable 3	propose 54
perform 69	poison 8	probably 116	prospect 34
performer 73	poisoned 24	problem 109	prospective 41
permission 77	poisonous 27	problems 114	protect 26
permit 78	poisons 33	proclaim 22	protecting 38
permitted 111	ponies 66	proclaimed 23	protection 26
permitting 93	pool 12	produce 43	protective 2
persisted 71	portable 3	produced 43	protector 103
pertain 69	portion 23	producing 47	proudly 24

Word List

WORD			LESSON
prove	22	reasonable	3	rejection	28	resist	68
proven	23	reasoning	11	relate	4	resisted	73
provide	106	rebuild	43	relation	41	resolve	36
proving	11	recapping	111	relationship	99	resolved	42
provision	52	receive	94	relative	27	resource	7
pulsate	82	receiver	112	relatives	111	resourceful	4
pulse	54	reception	26	relentless	98	respectable	42
puppies	54	receptive	24	relief	91	respectful	34
pure	83	record	118	relieve	92	respectfully	69
purist	83	recover	6	remarkable	6	rest	44
quest	16	recovered	42	remotely	107	restful	2
question	32	recreation	48	remoteness	116	restfully	19
questionable	31	recur	74	removal	39	resting	44
questions	27	recurred	114	remove	4	restless	1
quick	3	recurring	93	rental	12	restlessness	7
quickly	14	rediscover	42	repel	39	restoring	9
quiet	89	rediscovered	42	repelling	99	restrain	4
quotable	6	redissolve	42	replace	4	restrict	36
quote	4	reduce	44	replaces	97	restriction	44
racial	118	reduced	56	replacing	8	resume	97
racist	39	reducing	43	replied	86	resumed	117
raging	13	reduction	46	reply	86	resuming	99
rainiest	61	refer	51	report	6	retain	33
range	37	referring	97	reporter	111	retained	67
rather	19	refillable	7	repressive	24	retainer	104
ration	23	refine	62	request	19	retention	59
reach	33	refined	16	requested	48	return	4
reaches	28	reform	62	requesting	41	returnable	4
reacting	26	reformed	96	require	116	returning	7
reaction	27	refreshing	8	requirement	114	reusable	97
reactor	104	refusal	31	requirements	114	reversal	61
read	12	refuse	82	rerunning	98	reverse	68
readily	54	refused	62	resemble	107	revert	88
readiness	46	regard	43	resented	41	review	7
ready	41	regardless	48	reservation	109	reviewed	46
real	66	regress	26	reserve	6	reviewer	46
realistic	52	regressing	4	reserved	21	reviewing	46
really	14	reinstate	19	resign	47	revise	41
reappear	86	reject	27	resignation	111	revised	81
reason	1	rejecting	26	resigned	69	revision	43

Word List

WORD		LESSON

WORD	LESSON
rhythm	58
rhythmic	61
rhythmical	64
rhythmically	73
rich	9
riches	27
ridge	36
right	8
rights	38
ripen	61
ripeness	17
ripening	42
riper	17
ripest	11
river	113
robber	93
robbing	103
rocks	19
roofs	94
rope	102
round	28
roundly	74
ruling	12
run	8
runner	36
running	21
runny	26
sad	46
sadden	14
sadder	46
saddest	12
sadly	92
sadness	11
safest	17
sail	56
saint	68
saintly	69
sale	51
saltiest	83
salty	21
saw	78
saying	17
scales	113
scar	9
scarce	113
scariest	51
scary	88
scene	59
scenic	67
scenically	72
science	1
scientist	66
scientists	61
scope	64
scratch	36
scratches	118
scribe	9
script	14
scripts	27
scripture	31
sculpture	56
search	34
searches	36
seed	64
seeds	89
seek	12
seen	62
seize	28
seizure	28
self	77
selves	81
serve	3
serving	7
settle	21
settlement	23
several	109
sew	56
sewn	61
shake	64
shame	61
shamefully	63
shameless	9
shelf	76
she'll	49
shelves	79
shine	78
shiniest	34
shining	83
shipped	96
shipping	104
shoes	96
shop	52
shopper	13
shops	12
short	11
shortly	81
shouldn't	37
show	56
showed	52
shown	61
shrink	16
shrinkage	73
sign	9
signal	11
signature	82
silk	36
simple	41
simplest	47
simply	44
singing	7
sister	68
sketch	34
sketches	101
skidded	83
skidding	13
skillful	89
skills	19
skin	9
skinned	68
sleep	61
sleepiness	74
sleepless	3
sleeplessness	61
sleepy	89
sleeve	4
slick	38
slip	8
slipped	12
slipping	17
smiling	11
snapped	13
snapping	88
snappy	104
sneak	4
sneaky	89
snuggest	17
snugness	11
soften	53
softening	51
solve	7
solved	42
solving	8
some	4
soon	102
sore	4
soreness	8
sort	78
sound	4
sounded	8
source	3
sow	53
speak	28
speaker	103
speaks	88
speediest	38
speedily	83
speedy	21
spelling	104
spend	78
spent	3

Word List

WORD			LESSON
sphere................58	straining................7	suddenly................99	they................4
spherical................52	strayed................22	supplied................116	they'd................49
spin................34	strength................11	supplier................108	they'll................36
spinner................41	strengthen................36	supplies................98	they're................36
spinning................14	strengthening................39	supply................98	they've................37
spirit................22	stress................38	support................98	thick................34
spiritual................76	stressful................51	supports................117	thicken................44
spotless................12	stretch................27	suppose................98	thicker................44
spotted................18	stretcher................106	supposed................102	thickness................44
spotting................18	stretches................27	suppression................103	thief................42
spotty................34	strict................17	surface................98	thieves................78
sprays................38	strictly................19	surround................98	things................86
stack................37	structure................64	surrounded................102	think................38
stage................38	student................73	surroundings................108	thirst................22
staging................7	students................84	swim................3	thirsty................28
stance................117	studied................21	swimmer................13	this................74
star................8	studies................31	tail................8	thorough................73
starless................11	studious................29	taking................16	thoroughly................83
starred................18	studiously................37	tale................8	those................28
starring................13	studying................18	talked................114	thought................1
state................17	sturdiness................18	taxes................27	thoughtful................2
statement................22	style................34	teacher................13	thoughtless................1
station................41	stylish................44	tear................119	thousand................64
stay................14	stylishly................44	temper................83	thousands................97
stayed................19	subject................64	temperature................94	threaten................62
stays................31	submerge................64	temple................81	three................96
stepped................13	submerged................73	tempt................83	threw................9
stepping................12	submission................86	temptation................114	through................9
steps................21	submissive................77	tend................78	throughout................7
stopper................97	submitting................107	tense................17	throw................56
stopping................11	subscribe................64	tension................23	throwing................59
storage................18	subscription................67	tent................12	thrown................61
store................9	subsist................68	text................22	tighten................17
stored................11	substance................117	texture................24	tightening................66
stories................31	substantial................100	textured................93	time................114
stormiest................109	substantive................99	thank................37	timeless................7
storminess................71	subtract................67	that................67	tin................43
straight................21	subtraction................68	that's................37	to................9
straighten................17	subvert................88	their................8	today................47
strainer................94	subverted................99	there................8	tomorrow................48

Word List

WORD			LESSON
tone 14	trend 3	unknown 69	visual 81
too 9	trial 22	unlikely 87	voice 37
tough 11	trials 36	unrecorded 119	void 81
toughen 116	tribal 13	unrecovered 42	voters 78
tour 34	tribe 7	unreformed 19	wait 71
tourist 39	trick 36	unreported 18	wakening 67
toys 21	trickiest 52	unresolvable 17	walls 21
traced 7	tricks 99	unresolved 42	waltzes 28
tract 67	tried 17	unrevised 44	wandering 13
traction 67	tries 31	unsolved 42	want 54
tractor 104	trip 9	unstoppable 98	wash 27
tragic 54	trophies 66	unsurpassed ... 114	washes 27
tragically 72	trouble 102	until 74	washing 89
transact 64	troubling 103	unusual 88	wasn't 44
transaction 49	truck 34	use 1	water 8
transcribe 53	trucks 33	used 8	way 69
transfer 51	try 86	useful 8	ways 52
transferred .. 118	trying 19	useless 7	we 27
transferring ... 93	turned 8	uselessness 19	weak 88
transform 49	two 38	using 18	weakness 6
transfusion 82	type 34	usual 76	wear 18
transgression . 51	typical 44	usually 79	weather 9
transgressor . 104	typist 57	valuable 9	week 91
translated 56	unapproved 71	value 9	weight 68
translation 52	unbreakable ... 28	varied 23	we'll 36
transmission . 77	unconfirmed ... 19	varies 33	went 48
transmit 78	uncover 9	various 37	were 4
transmitter ... 94	uncovered 42	variously 37	we're 37
transplant 67	under 64	vary 8	weren't 13
transport 49	undiscovered .. 42	vast 83	we've 41
transportation 93	undissolved 42	vastly 88	what's 49
trap 34	unexpected 37	vein 3	where 18
trapped 12	unfair 9	venture 57	whether 9
trapper 24	unfairness 9	ventured 64	which 16
trapping 89	unfounded 36	verse 14	while 61
trays 54	unhappy 9	very 8	whole 8
treasure 48	unhurried 109	view 2	who's 37
treasures 54	unintended 64	views 118	whose 32
treat 17	union 31	vision 41	widely 14
treatment 22	unions 36	visor 107	wideness 29

Word List

WORD			LESSON
widest 12	wolf 76	worry 14	write 8
wife 77	wolves 78	worth 1	writer 109
wild 89	wonder 9	worthiness 109	writing 53
win 3	wonderful 12	worthless 1	wrong 1
wind 96	wood 9	worthy 66	year 24
winner 13	workable 3	would 9	yesterday 47
wishes 54	worldly 17	wouldn't 88	you 23
with 27	worried 22	wrap 43	you'll 49
without 1	worrier 17	wrapping 89	your 27
wives 78	worries 31	wreckage 18	youthfulness 7

Study Lists

1–5

base
breakable
cover
cure
doubt
doubtful
fresh
guide
helpless
like
match
matchless
misfile
misjudge
mismatch
misplace
misquote
misshape
misspell
misuse
mother
move
name
painful
place
pointless
portable
power
powerful
powerless
price
print
quote
reason
reasonable
relate
remove
resourceful
restful
restrain
return
returnable
serve
sleepless
sore
sound
thought
thoughtless
view
workable
worth
worthless

6–10

athletes
breath
brightness
cheerful
curable
doubting
exercised
fair
fairness
faithful
fashion
fashionable
fearful
feat
feet
firmness
globe
guided
guiding
having
hear
helped
helplessness
here
hole
hopeless
hoping
kindness
likable
liked
likeness
loan
lone
misspelling
morning
named
nineteen
painfulness
peace
piece
priceless
pricing
quotable
recover
refillable
refreshing
remarkable
replace
replacing
report
reserve
resource
restlessness
restoring
returning
review
rich
right
scribe
serving
shameless
sign
singing
solve
solving
soreness
sounded
source
staging
store
straining
tail
tale
their
there
thoughtful
threw
through
throughout
timeless
to
too
traced
tribe
turned
uncover
unfair
unfairness
unhappy
used
useless
valuable
value
vary
very
weakness
weather
whether
whole
wood
would
write
youthfulness

11–15

biggest
coolest
darker
darkest
doubtless
dropper
farmer
final
finer
firm
flatly
flatness
formal
fresher
fright
frost
global
greatest
helper
hopeful
hopping
interested
length
lifeless
lighter
loose
madness
mothering
part
people
photograph
placing
planned
proving

Study Lists

quickly
raging
really
reasoning
rental
ripest
sadden
saddest
sadness
script
short
signal
skidding
slipped
smiling
snapped
snugness
spinning
spotless
starless
starring
stepped
stepping
stopping
stored
strength
swimmer
teacher
tone
tough
trapped
tribal
verse
wandering
weren't
widely
widest
winner
wonderful

16–20

anybody
ate
barred
boats
carried
carrying
change
claim
confine
conform
confronted
conserve
crease
creased
create
darken
defining
delight
delights
departed
deport
describe
drying
eight
fanciest
finely
finest
frightening
govern
happiness
healthy
helplessly
hiding
hoped
inborn
inhuman
inland
instead

largest
lonely
loosely
loosen
madder
madly
meat
meet
misreported
nastiest
package
peaceful
pitiful
pitying
playful
playing
press
quest
rather
refined
reinstate
restfully
ripeness
riper
rocks
safest
saying
shrink
skills
slipping
snuggest
spotted
spotting
starred
starring
state
storage
straighten
strict
studying

sturdiness
taking
tense
tighten
treat
tried
unconfirmed
unreformed
unresolvable
uselessness
using
which
worldly
worrier
wreckage

21–25

action
active
agree
cause
changing
clapping
confinement
context
crying
deforming
denial
detecting
easy
edgy
exchange
exchanging
explain
express
facing
feature
found
government

great
hurried
increasing
kings
lately
lights
lowest
lucky
massive
nastier
passion
passive
poisoned
portion
pressure
proclaim
proclaimed
profile
profound
progress
proudly
prove
proven
ration
receptive
repressive
reserved
running
salty
settle
settlement
speedy
spirit
statement
steps
straight
strayed
studied
tension
text

Study Lists

texture
thirst
toys
trapper
treatment
trial
varied
walls
worried

26–30

boxes
brushes
buzzes
claims
concept
conjecture
danger
defeated
dejected
depression
detect
detective
duty
except
expressed
expression
famous
featuring
fineness
fitness
flawed
furious
fury
glorious
happiest
happily
injected
injection
invaluable

joyous
lower
maddest
matches
misconception
movement
notion
passes
poisonous
preschool
preserve
presses
preview
profoundly
progressed
progression
progressive
project
protect
protection
protective
reaches
reaction
reception
regress
reject
rejecting
rejection
relative
riches
round
runny
seize
seizure
shops
speak
stretch
studious
taxes
thirsty
unexpected

waltzes
wash
wideness

31–35

actively
babies
beautiful
beauty
berries
black
boys
bridge
cage
carries
cities
contain
copies
count
cries
dangerous
deception
detain
detection
development
dress
duties
edginess
exception
flies
fork
friendliness
furiously
furry
hedge
inspect
inspection
joys
judge
large

latch
logic
loneliest
maintain
major
nice
noisily
order
park
physical
pinches
plays
pleasure
poisons
projecting
projection
prospect
questionable
reach
refusal
respectful
retain
science
scripture
search
shiniest
sketch
spin
spotty
stays
stories
studies
style
think
tour
tries
truck
trucks
type
union
worries

36–40

aren't
artist
batch
can't
catches
class
cloudiness
container
couldn't
dangerously
denies
disarm
discharged
discounts
discovering
disease
dislike
dispel
displeasing
ditch
doggy
don't
dresses
dries
easiest
exceptional
expel
force
forcefully
fuss
getting
glasses
gloriously
here's
hurries
increasingly
intention
joyously
kick

Study Lists

largely
ledge
let's
look
nervous
nervously
patch
placement
player
pledge
progressively
propel
range
removal
repel
ridge
scratch
searches
scientist
shouldn't
silk
speediest
sprays
stack
strengthening
stretches
studiously
thank
that's
they'll
they're
they've
think
tourist
trials
trick
unexpected
unions
varies
various
variously

voice
we'll
we're
who's

41–45

artistic
basic
beautifully
bought
brief
build
building
chance
chief
chiefly
childish
committee
conception
courage
creation
cross
crosses
deceptive
deduce
departure
descriptive
devise
didn't
discover
discovered
disrespect
dissolving
ditches
doesn't
foolish
graphic
grief
heavy
heroic

high
honesty
I've
kind
kindest
kindly
misplaced
misshapen
niece
photography
produce
produced
prospective
question
ready
rediscovered
reduce
reducing
regard
relation
requesting
resented
resolve
resolved
respectable
rest
resting
restless
restriction
revise
revision
ripening
simple
spinner
star
station
stylish
stylishly
thick
thicken
thicker

thickness
thief
typical
undiscovered
unrecovered
unresolved
unrevised
vision
we've

46–50

afternoon
boyish
classical
close
clothes
conduct
conducted
creative
designer
discourage
edging
evening
explorers
forceful
intensively
island
it's
magic
nieces
producing
product
productive
readiness
recreation
reduction
regardless
requested
resign
she'll

simplest
some
they'd
today
tomorrow
transaction
transform
transport
treasure
what's
yesterday
you'll

51–55

athletic
benches
bodies
cleanliness
comic
confer
conquests
critic
critical
defer
depose
deserve
design
discouragement
disgraceful
disorder
disposal
dispose
evenings
expose
finally
finish
finished
inflamed
intensive
losses

Study Lists

medic
misinformed
monkeys
pain
peacefully
prefer
prescribe
prescription
production
propose
provision
pulse
puppies
readily
realistic
refer
request
sale
scariest
soften
softening
sow /ō/
spherical
stressful
tragic
transcribe
transfer
transgression
translation
trays
trickiest
wishes

56–60

appoint
appraisal
appraise
approve
blow
chancy
comical
content
convention
cycle
draw
exposure
expressive
extent
grow
hurrying
invent
invention
know
prevent
proposal
reduced
retention
rhythm
sail
scene
sculpture
sew
show
sphere
throw
translated
typist
venture

61–65

accident
appointment
assistants
automobile
blown
construct
contend
contents
define
deform
description
destruction
disclosure
dishonest
disposable
drawn
easily
extend
extended
extension
forbid
forget
forgive
forgiven
golden
ground
grown
hottest
instruct
intend
intentional
known
merge
pretend
prevention
rainiest
refine
reform
reversal
rhythmic
rhythmical
ripen
scientists
seen
sewn
shame
shamefully
shopper
shown
sleep
sleeplessness
strengthen
structure
subject
submerge
subscribe
threaten
thrown
unintended
ventured
while

66–70

assistant
brother
carelessly
cheerfulness
consist
construction
contract
crashes
cubic
cyclist
extract
failure
false
falsely
flattest
forgetful
forgiving
foxes
friendliest
grounds
habit
insist
insisted
instruction
lengthen
lilies
liveliness
object
objective
observe
obtain
obtained
payment
peaches
perception
perform
pertain
ponies
pound
pretending
resigned
resist
respectfully
retained
reverse
saint
sister
skinned
subsist
subtract
subtraction
tightening
tract
traction
transplant
trophies
unbreakable
wakening
weight
worthy

71–75

aground
alike
along
apart
appears
around
athletically
awaken
basically
classically

Study Lists

comically
complain
compose
compress
compression
concur
conscientious
contentment
costly
critically
cubically
defective
delightful
distraction
extraction
firmly
graphically
heroically
incur
infect
infection
instructional
likely
logically
magically
nicely
objection
oblong
observer
observing
perceptive
perfect
perfection
performer
persisted
physically
recur
resisted
rhythmically
roundly
scenically

sleepiness
storminess
strictly
student
submerged
thorough
tragically
unapproved
wait

76–80

across
alone
apiece
bear
boyhood
calf
childhood
commission
commissioner
commit
compile
contraction
defrosting
destructive
dismiss
factual
falsehood
globally
gradual
habitual
half
halves
imperfect
knife
leaf
leaves
life
likelihood
loaf

loaves
mission
motherhood
objectionable
permission
permit
self
shelf
shelves
spiritual
submissive
thieves
transmission
transmit
usual
usually
wife
wives
wolf
wolves

81–85

activate
appear
avoidable
bare
calves
composure
confuse
confusion
conservation
defuse
designate
elves
ethically
explorer
friend
image
immobile
informative

knives
medicate
mobile
obstruction
please
proper
properly
pulsate
pure
refuse
revised
selves
shortly
signature
temper
temple
tempt
thoroughly
transfusion
vast
visual
void

86–90

acquiring
activation
applied
applies
apply
approach
avoiding
because
behave
belong
belongs
beside
casual
comply
confusing
contempt

convert
describing
devastating
fascinates
impart
imply
import
improve
invert
knowledge
livelihood
medication
observation
orderly
reappear
replied
reply
revert
speaks
submission
subvert
unlikely
weak

91–95

acquire
adequately
adjust
admit
advise
avoided
befriended
behaved
belief
beliefs
believable
believe
challenge
chiefs
cliffs

Study Lists

conceive
contention
convent
conversation
converse
conversion
converted
deceive
decompression
disbelief
eject
emerge
environment
evaluate
event
eventual
gulfs
imported
improperly
improved
improvement
incurable
intent
inverse
inversion
inverted
lives
perceive
permitting
preferred
protecting
receive
recurring
relief
robber
roofs
sadly
strainer
temperature
textured
transferring

transmitter
transportation
unusual
week

96–100

address
adjusted
adjustment
admission
adventure
committed
compelling
completely
constant
constrained
consume
consumer
contemplate
courtship
desert
educate
emerged
eventful
friendship
hardship
implied
incomplete
instant
instantly
opposed
outfitted
perfectly
photographs
presume
propeller
referring
reformed
relationship
relentless
repelling

rerunning
resume
resuming
shipped
stopper
substantial
substantive
supplies
supply
support
suppose
surface
surround
unstoppable

101–105

actor
addictive
attain
attest
attract
became
brought
champion
character
citizen
composer
compressor
cutting
defection
defector
demote
dessert
dictate
disarmed
dissect
emotion
factions
factor
families
family

insect
instructor
interaction
intercept
intermission
intersect
interview
interviewed
inventor
motive
photographer
planter
predict
projector
prominent
promote
protector
reactor
retainer
robbing
shipping
snappy
speaker
subverted
supposed
suppression
surrounded
tractor
transgressor
trouble
troubling
unknown

106–110

admitted
attractive
commitment
concise
conduction
conductor
confession

considered
contractor
decisive
dictation
dictator
distant
divide
division
education
educator
expelled
foreign
forgotten
gripped
heavier
incision
inquire
instructive
intersection
marry
misspeller
nations
precise
prediction
problem
profess
profession
professor
promoter
promotion
provide
remotely
resemble
reservation
several
stormiest
submitting
unhurried
visor
worthiness
writer

Study Lists

111–115

attempt
attention
bound
cave
custom
decisions
district
divided
grave
individual
information
inspector
interviewer
inventive
legend
merry
motivate
permitted
prime
professional
promoted
recapping
recurred
reporter
requirement
requirements
resignation
scarce
temptation
unsurpassed

116–120

attraction
bushes
commotion
compelled
competition
confrontation
continue
delightfully
dictionary
distance
distressing
exploration
facial
forgetting
inquiry
instance
married
necessary
partial
partially
precisely
preservation
probably
racial
record
remoteness
require
resumed
reviewer
scratches
substance
supplied
toughen
transferred
unrecorded
views

Spelling Rules

Lesson	Rule	Explanation
6	Final-E Rule	When do you drop the final **e** from a word? When the next morphograph begins with a vowel letter.
11	Doubling Rule (Short Words)	When do you double the final **c** in a short word? When the word ends **cvc** and the next morphograph begins with **v**.
16	Y-to-I Rule	When do you change the **y** to **i** in a word? When the word ends with a consonant-and-**y** and the next morphograph begins with anything except **i**.
22	W as a Vowel	When is **w** a vowel letter? At the end of a morphograph.
23	Y as a Vowel	When is **y** a vowel letter? At the end of a morphograph.
26	E-S Endings	If a word ends in **s, z, sh,** or **ch,** you add **e-s** to make the plural word.
27	E-S Endings X as Two Consonant Letters	If a word ends in **x,** you add **e-s** to make the plural word. The letter **x** acts like two consonants because it has two consonant sounds.
31	E-S Endings	If a word ends with a consonant-and-**y,** you add **e-s** to make the plural word.
61	E-N Variation	If a word ends with the letter **w** and you add **e-n,** drop the **e**.
71	A-L Insertion	When a word ends in the letters **i-c,** you add the morphograph **a-l** before adding **l-y**.
78	/ff/ Endings	Some words that end in the sound **/ff/** have the letters **v-e-s** in the plural.
93	Doubling Rule (Long Words)	When the word ends in a short **cvc** morphograph, use the doubling rule.
103	O-R Endings	If a form of the word ends in **i-o-n,** use **o-r**.

Meanings of Affixes and Nonword Bases

Morphograph	Lesson	Meanings	Examples
a-	71	in, on, at; not, without	ahead; apart, atypical
-able	3	can be	stretchable, washable, readable
ad-	94	to, toward; against	advise, adjustment; adverse
-age	18	result of an action	package, usage, marriage
-al	12	related to, like	formal, trial, rental
ap-	56	to, toward, against	appointment, approval, appendage
-ary	118	related to; connected to	dictionary, library, secondary
at-	104	to, toward, against	attract, attention, attest
-ate	82	to make, act on; having the quality of	evaluate, activate; passionate
be-	86	to make; over; really	became, beside, because
ceive	94	to take; contain	receiver, conceive, deceived
cept	24	to take; contain	receptive, intercept, acceptable
cise	108	to cut	incision, concise, precisely
com-	73	with, together	compress, combat, commission
con-	19	with, together	conform, contest, condense
cord	118	rope; heart; in agreement	cording; record, accord, cordial
cur	74	to run, to happen	concur, recurred, current

Meanings of Affixes and Nonword Bases

Morphograph	Lesson	Meanings	Examples
de-	16	down, away from; reverse of; remove from	deport, deform, depart
di-	107	twice; through, across	divert, divide, direct
dict	104	to speak; to fix	predict, diction
dis-	37	opposite of; not; completely	dispel, discount, disease
duce	43	to lead	produce, educate, reducing
duct	46	to lead	productive, conductor, deductive
e-	92	missing out, away	eject, emitted, event
-ed	8	[action] in the past	formed, stepped, cried
-en	17	to make	loosen, darken, straighten
-er	13	more; one who	greater, lighter; teacher, dancer
-es	26	more than one; a verb marker for he, she, or it	lilies, boxes; watches, catches
-est	11	the most	greatest, lightest, happiest
ex-	21	out, away	export, exclude, extend
fect	72	to do, to make	defective, confection, perfect
fer	51	to carry	transfer, infer, referred
fess	106	to speak	profess, confession, professor
for-	63	against, completely	forbid, forgotten, forgiving
-ful	2	full of; tending to	careful, beautiful; forgetful
fuse	82	to pour or melt	transfusion, confusion
gress	24	to step	regression, progress, transgression
-hood	77	state, quality	motherhood, likelihood, childhood

Meanings of Affixes and Nonword Bases

Morphograph	Lesson	Meanings	Examples
-ial	118	related to, like	partial, facial, adverbial
-ic	43	like, related to	basic, typically, artistic
im-	87	in, into; not	impose, impression, impurity
in-	18	in, into; not; really	include; incurable; invaluable
-ing	7	when you do something, ongoing action	spending, moving, stopping
inter-	101	between	interact, intersect, intervention
-ion	23	state, quality, act, or process	action, taxation, repression
-ish	44	like, related to, inclined to be	babyish, stylish, boyish, greenish
-ist	39	one who	artist, typist, tourist
-ive	23	quality of; one who	expressive, informative; relative, detective
ject	26	to throw	rejecting, dejected, projection
-less	1	without	painless, useless, restless
lief	91	to lift, allow	belief, disbelief, relief
lieve	92	to lift, allow	believe, believable
-ly	14	how something is done	quietly, equally, basically
-ment	22	result of doing something	placement, requirement, apartment
mis-	1	wrongly	misspell, misjudge, misprint
miss	77	to send	admission, dismiss, missile
mit	78	to send	transmit, admitted, commitment

Meanings of Affixes and Nonword Bases

Meanings of Affixes and Nonword Bases

Morphograph	Lesson	Meanings	Examples
mote	103	to move	motionless, demote, promotional
-ness	6	that which is, quality of	thickness, quietness, freshness
ob-	67	to, toward, against	obstruct, obtain, objection
-ous	27	having the quality of	famous, furious, joyous
pel	39	to push	expel, propeller, repellent
per	69	through	perform, pertain, perceive
ply	86	a layer; to fold; full	pliable; comply; supplier
pose	54	to act a certain way; to put, to place	position, composure, opposite
pre-	26	before	preview, preclude, prepay
pro-	22	in favor of; before; forward	proclaim; provision; progress
quest	16	to seek, to ask for	conquest, request, questionable
quire	107	to seek, to ask for	inquire, requirement, acquire
re-	4	again, back	rerun, return, replace
-s	19	more than one; a verb marker for *he, she,* or *it*	friends, bananas, farmers; acts, writes, talks
sect	102	to cut	section, dissect, intersect
semble	107	same; together	resemble; assemble, ensemble
-ship	97	state, quality	friendship, hardship, relationship
sist	68	to stand, to set, to make	persist, resist, consists
spect	34	to look	inspect, respect, perspective

Meanings of Affixes and Nonword Bases

Morphograph	Lesson	Meanings	Examples
stance	117	to stand, to set	instance, substance, distance
stant	99	to stand, to set	constant, substantive, instant
struct	64	to build	structure, destruction, constructive
sub-	64	under	subtract, subhuman, submission
sume	97	to take	consumer, resume, presumable
sup-	98	under	support, suppressed, supposed
tain	33	to hold	retaining, container, detained
tect	24	to cover	detecting, protection
tend	62	to be inclined to; to stretch	attend, intend; extend
tent	59	to hold	content, attention, intent
tract	67	to drag, to draw	tractor, attractive, subtraction
trans-	49	across	transportation, transform, transfer
-ual	76	related to, like	factual, usual, gradual
un-	9	not, the opposite	unhappy, unusual, untie
-ure	24	act, process	departure, pressure, failure
vent	57	to come	prevent, invention, adventure
vert	88	to turn	invert, convert, introvert
vide	106	to see; to separate	providing; divide, individual
vise	41	to see; to separate	advise, visual; division
-y	21	having the quality of; belonging to	shiny, dreamy, mighty

Contractions

Component Words	Contractions
are not	aren't
can not	can't
could not	couldn't
did not	didn't
do not	don't
does not	doesn't
have not	haven't
he had	he'd
he is	he's
he will	he'll
here is	here's
I am	I'm
I have	I've
I will	I'll
it is	it's
let us	let's
she had	she'd
she is	she's
she will	she'll

Component Words	Contractions
should not	shouldn't
that is	that's
they are	they're
they had	they'd
they have	they've
they will	they'll
was not	wasn't
we are	we're
we had	we'd
we have	we've
we will	we'll
were not	weren't
what is	what's
who is	who's
would not	wouldn't
you are	you're
you had	you'd
you will	you'll

Homonyms

ate	refers to: eat in the past example: I *ate* a sandwich.	for	refers to: in place of example: She went to the store *for* me.
eight	refers to: the number 8 example: The dog had *eight* puppies.	four	refers to: the number 4 example: Cats have *four* legs.
bare	refers to: without covering; empty example: In the winter some trees are *bare*.	hear	refers to: listen example: I can't *hear* you.
bear	refers to: a certain animal, or to support example: The huge *bear* drank from a stream. example: The bridge can't *bear* more weight.	here	refers to: this place example: Come over *here*.
		hole	refers to: empty space example: I have a *hole* in my sock.
		whole	refers to: entire, complete example: He ate the *whole* pie.
close	refers to: shut something example: Please *close* the door.	loan	refers to: allow to borrow something example: She will *loan* me lunch money.
clothes	refers to: things you wear example: They bought lots of *clothes*.	lone	refers to: by itself example: There was a *lone* tree.
desert	refers to: leave or abandon example: I wouldn't *desert* a friend in need.	marry	refers to: wed or unite example: She said she would *marry* Steve.
dessert	refers to: food served at the end of a meal example: We had ice cream for *dessert*.	merry	refers to: happy, full of fun example: The hikers were a *merry* group.
feat	refers to: something hard to do example: Climbing the mountain was a great *feat*.	meat	refers to: food from animals example: Some people don't eat *meat*.
feet	refers to: body part example: Her *feet* were sore from running.	meet	refers to: come together example: We agreed to *meet* next week.

Homonyms 211

Homonyms

no	refers to: negative answer example: *No*, I'm not going.	**sew**	refers to: join with a needle and thread example: He will *sew* a new button on his coat.
know	refers to: understand or be familiar with example: We *know* how to sail.	**sow**	refers to: plant seeds example: Farmers *sow* their fields in the early spring.
peace	refers to: calm; no war example: I like *peace* and quiet.	**tail**	refers to: the back end example: The dog chased his *tail*.
piece	refers to: a part example: I ate a *piece* of fruit.	**tale**	refers to: a story. example: He told an interesting *tale*.
plain	refers to: simple; ordinary example: She wore a *plain* black dress.	**their**	refers to: belonging to them example: It is *their* house.
plane	refers to: flat surface; air transportation example: The *plane* landed safely.	**there**	refers to: that place example: Go over *there*.
right	refers to: correct; opposite of left example: All my answers were *right*. example: She wears a ring on her *right* hand.	**they're**	refers to: they are example: I think *they're* ready.
write	refers to: put words on paper example: You must *write* neatly.	**threw**	refers to: throw in the past example: She *threw* the ball.
sail	refers to: travel on water in a ship or a boat example: We learned how to *sail* at camp.	**through**	refers to: in one side and out the other example: We went *through* the tunnel.
sale	refers to: available to buy; an offer at a cheaper price example: Our house is for *sale*. He bought the shoes on *sale*.	**to**	refers to: at or toward example: She walked *to* school.
scene	refers to: view or setting example: It was a painting of an ocean *scene*.	**too**	refers to: also example: Why don't you come along, *too*?
seen	refers to: see in the past example: I have *seen* that picture.	**two**	refers to: the number 2 example: I ate *two* apples.

Homonyms

vary	refers to: change example: His moods *vary* from day to day.	**weak**	refers to: the opposite of strong example: The wrestler felt *weak* after the match.
very	refers to: really, quite, especially example: That story is *very* imaginative.	**week**	refers to: seven days example: We go on vacation next *week*.
wait	refers to: delay; expect something example: We had to *wait* an hour for the bus.	**wood**	refers to: what trees are made of example: We need *wood* for the fire.
weight	refers to: heaviness example: He felt like he had the *weight* of the world on his shoulders.	**would**	refers to: what might happen example: I *would* like to go to Paris.
wear	refers to: have clothes on your body example: What shall I *wear* today?	**your**	refers to: belonging to you example: *Your* coat is blue.
where	refers to: what place example: *Where* do you want to go?	**you're**	refers to: you are example: *You're* early.
weather	refers to: what it feels like out of doors example: Always wear a hat in cold *weather*.		
whether	refers to: if example: I don't care *whether* I go or not.		

Homonyms

Short-Vowel, Long-Vowel Spelling Patterns

an   en   in   on   un

Part A		
badge	budge	range
edge	fudge	fringe
hedge	judge	sponge
ledge	nudge	barge
pledge	trudge	large
sledge	page	age
ridge	rage	cage
bridge	stage	huge
dodge	wage	
lodge	change	

Part C		
press	kiss	choice
bliss	boss	voice
dress	loss	once
grass	gloss	fence
miss	moss	since
class	toss	dance
glass	fuss	place
pass	cross	ice
bless	trace	nice
mess	race	mice
stress	face	chance
hiss	force	

Part B		
back	thick	dark
sack	shock	park
tack	rock	fork
stack	lock	desk
black	block	mask
track	knock	break
neck	clock	thank
deck	luck	cheek
speck	stuck	walk
pick	duck	bank
sick	truck	sulk
kick	silk	bunk
slick	milk	sank
trick	think	

Part D		
latch	witch	bench
match	switch	drench
catch	snatch	inch
batch	scratch	pinch
hatch	scotch	launch
patch	notch	bunch
fetch	blotch	crunch
stretch	clutch	arch
sketch	crutch	search
itch	reach	church
ditch	teach	pouch
pitch	coach	touch
stitch	speech	

Test Charts

	Lesson 5	Lesson 10	Lesson 15	Lesson 20	Lesson 25	Lesson 30	
Super Speller	25	25	25	25	25	25	**30-Lesson Total**
	24	24	24	24	24	24	
	23	23	23	23	23	23	
Very Good Speller	22	22	22	22	22	22	138 = Super Speller
	21	21	21	21	21	21	
	20	20	20	20	20	20	
	19	19	19	19	19	19	
	18	18	18	18	18	18	
	17	17	17	17	17	17	
	16	16	16	16	16	16	
	15	15	15	15	15	15	
	14	14	14	14	14	14	
	13	13	13	13	13	13	
	12	12	12	12	12	12	
	11	11	11	11	11	11	
	10	10	10	10	10	10	
	9	9	9	9	9	9	
	8	8	8	8	8	8	
	7	7	7	7	7	7	
	6	6	6	6	6	6	
	5	5	5	5	5	5	
	4	4	4	4	4	4	
	3	3	3	3	3	3	
	2	2	2	2	2	2	
	1	1	1	1	1	1	

Test Charts

	Lesson 35	Lesson 40	Lesson 45	Lesson 50	Lesson 55	Lesson 60	
Super Speller	25	25	25	25	25	25	**30-Lesson Total**
	24	24	24	24	24	24	
	23	23	23	23	23	23	
Very Good Speller	22	22	22	22	22	22	**138 = Super Speller**
	21	21	21	21	21	21	
	20	20	20	20	20	20	
	19	19	19	19	19	19	
	18	18	18	18	18	18	
	17	17	17	17	17	17	
	16	16	16	16	16	16	
	15	15	15	15	15	15	
	14	14	14	14	14	14	
	13	13	13	13	13	13	
	12	12	12	12	12	12	
	11	11	11	11	11	11	
	10	10	10	10	10	10	
	9	9	9	9	9	9	
	8	8	8	8	8	8	
	7	7	7	7	7	7	
	6	6	6	6	6	6	
	5	5	5	5	5	5	
	4	4	4	4	4	4	
	3	3	3	3	3	3	
	2	2	2	2	2	2	
	1	1	1	1	1	1	

Test Charts

	Lesson 65	Lesson 70	Lesson 75	Lesson 80	Lesson 85	Lesson 90	
Super Speller	25	25	25	25	25	25	**30-Lesson Total**
	24	24	24	24	24	24	
	23	23	23	23	23	23	
Very Good Speller	22	22	22	22	22	22	**138 = Super Speller**
	21	21	21	21	21	21	
	20	20	20	20	20	20	
	19	19	19	19	19	19	
	18	18	18	18	18	18	
	17	17	17	17	17	17	
	16	16	16	16	16	16	
	15	15	15	15	15	15	
	14	14	14	14	14	14	
	13	13	13	13	13	13	
	12	12	12	12	12	12	
	11	11	11	11	11	11	
	10	10	10	10	10	10	
	9	9	9	9	9	9	
	8	8	8	8	8	8	
	7	7	7	7	7	7	
	6	6	6	6	6	6	
	5	5	5	5	5	5	
	4	4	4	4	4	4	
	3	3	3	3	3	3	
	2	2	2	2	2	2	
	1	1	1	1	1	1	

Test Charts

	Lesson 95	Lesson 100	Lesson 105	Lesson 110	Lesson 115	Lesson 120	
Super Speller	25	25	25	25	25	25	**30-Lesson Total**
	24	24	24	24	24	24	
	23	23	23	23	23	23	
Very Good Speller	22	22	22	22	22	22	**138 = Super Speller**
	21	21	21	21	21	21	
	20	20	20	20	20	20	
	19	19	19	19	19	19	
	18	18	18	18	18	18	
	17	17	17	17	17	17	
	16	16	16	16	16	16	
	15	15	15	15	15	15	
	14	14	14	14	14	14	
	13	13	13	13	13	13	
	12	12	12	12	12	12	
	11	11	11	11	11	11	
	10	10	10	10	10	10	
	9	9	9	9	9	9	
	8	8	8	8	8	8	
	7	7	7	7	7	7	
	6	6	6	6	6	6	
	5	5	5	5	5	5	
	4	4	4	4	4	4	
	3	3	3	3	3	3	
	2	2	2	2	2	2	
	1	1	1	1	1	1	